D0815936

*Third Parties*
*in*
*Presidential Elections*

☆

*Daniel A. Mazmanian*

☆

# *Third Parties*
# *in*
# *Presidential Elections*

*Studies in Presidential Selection*

THE BROOKINGS INSTITUTION

*Washington, D.C.*

*Copyright © 1974 by*
THE BROOKINGS INSTITUTION
*1775 Massachusetts Avenue, N.W., Washington, D.C. 20036*

*Library of Congress Cataloging in Publication Data:*

Mazmanian, Daniel A    1945–
  Third parties in presidential elections.
  (Studies in presidential selection)
  Includes bibliographical references.
    1. Third parties (United States—Politics)
2. Presidents—United States—Election.    I. Title.
II. Series.
JK2261.M38    329'.02    74-281
ISBN 0-8157-5522-8
ISBN 0-8157-5521-x (pbk.)

1 2 3 4 5 6 7 8 9

# Foreword

TWO-PARTY COMPETITION is usual in American politics. Yet important third parties have emerged in presidential contests fairly often. Their relative power is underscored by the nearly 10 million votes cast for George C. Wallace and the American Independent party in 1968. The absence of a large third-party vote in 1972 did little to dampen the interest in third parties that the 1968 election aroused. The potential for the resurgence of the AIP persists as does the possibility that new movements will arise on the political left or right. Since third parties are viewed by some as inimical to the American electoral system, it is appropriate that their origins, their impact on public policy and on the party system, and their episodic nature be examined.

Daniel A. Mazmanian, a research associate at Brookings, discusses the leading third parties that have contended for the presidency over the last 140 years. His analysis reveals the conditions necessary for significant third-party voting and the effects of third parties on presidential elections, the party system, and public policy. He believes that more nearly permanent minor parties would enrich the presidential contest, and he recommends a national election code that would ensure the survival of strong minor parties. He does not foresee a great proliferation of new political parties in a broadened party system, but he does expect the complexion of the traditional two-party system to change. His conclusions should be informative and provocative for those attempting to understand and evaluate third parties in American politics.

The author and the Institution are grateful to the many students of American politics who provided advice during the preparation of the book. A bipartisan public advisory council, a list of whose members precedes this foreword, offered practical comment on this study as it does on each volume in the Studies in Presidential Selection series. A small group of scholars who met at Brookings in July 1972 contributed suggestions that have been considered in subsequent revision; their names, and their affiliations at the time of the conference, are listed at the end of the text. Gilbert Y. Steiner, director of Governmental Studies at Brookings, and Donald R. Matthews, under whose general supervision this and other studies in presidential selection have been carried out, were helpful throughout the planning, research, and writing of the book. The manuscript benefited from comments by Herbert Kaufman, William R. Keech, Judith H. Parris, Michael Rogin, James L. Sundquist, and several anonymous readers. Stuart K. Witt was of invaluable assistance in the preparation of the chapter on the modified party system. Alice M. Carroll edited the manuscript and Avima Ruder prepared the index. Sara Sklar and Delores Burton typed the several drafts.

This book is the sixth in the Brookings series of Studies in Presidential Selection. Financial support for the project of which this book is a part was furnished by a grant from the Ford Foundation. The views, opinions, and interpretations in the book are those of the author and should not be attributed to other staff members, officers, or trustees of the Brookings Institution or to the Ford Foundation.

KERMIT GORDON
*President*

*February 1974*
*Washington, D.C.*

# Contents

*Third Parties*
*in*
*Presidential Elections*

☆

*Chapter One*

☆

# THE WALLACE PHENOMENON
# IN A TWO-PARTY SYSTEM

THE AMERICAN two-party system stems from the nation's cultural values and electoral institutions. It is a system that has been strengthened by experience. Strong, active, and persistent minorities, holding views diametrically opposed to those of most Americans, have not developed in the United States.[1] The Constitution, the governmental framework, the regulated but largely free-enterprise capitalist economy, and the pattern of social status are seldom challenged. Instead, politics has most often been concerned with divisions over secondary issues that are more susceptible to negotiation and compromise. This "liberal tradition"[2] has enabled the nation to avoid the frequent confrontations over fundamentals that have led to irreconcilable political conflicts in European nations. For Americans, "the price of union" has been avoiding conflict over fundamentals;[3] political factions thus can coalesce around pragmatic issues within the two major parties.

The oppositions that have developed as issues surfaced within the society have lent themselves to two-party alignments: division over adoption of the Constitution, and the Federalism-Jeffersonian

1. See Daniel J. Boorstin, *The Genius of American Politics* (University of Chicago Press, 1953); Richard Hofstadter, *The American Political Tradition* (Knopf, 1948); and Sidney Hyman, *The Politics of Consensus* (Random House, 1968).

2. Louis Hartz, *The Liberal Tradition in America* (Harcourt, Brace and World, 1955).

3. Herbert Agar, *The Price of Union* (2nd ed., Houghton Mifflin, 1966).

alignment dominant throughout the formative stages of the party system;[4] the split between North and South in the Civil War era; and in recent decades the urban-rural, labor-management, and social class divisions.[5]

The binding element in two-partyism, however, is the winner-take-all arrangement in the electoral arena.[6] Deciding elections by a plurality vote in single-member districts rather than proportional representation assures there is only one victor. Those seeking the rewards of office are encouraged to coalesce to gain victory.[7] The losing party, with the prospect of a possible future victory, becomes the rallying point for opposition groups. Third parties rarely have the potential for victory and are thus encouraged to join with one of the leading parties in hopes of becoming part of a winning coalition.[8]

The single-member district, although sufficient to account for the formation of two parties in each election district,[9] does not explain the presence of the two national parties. Competition for the presidency explains their durability.[10] The formation of national coalitions, extending across the fifty states, in pursuit of the presidency has led many factions not only to compromise but also to transcend ideology. This drive to form a winning coalition tends to reduce the final number of competitors in the presidential race to two. As in single-member-district contests, the runner-up usually survives because of the promise of future victories, and third parties have little prospect of success.

4. V. O. Key, Jr., *Politics, Parties, and Pressure Groups* (5th ed., Crowell, 1964), p. 207.

5. James C. Charlesworth, "Is Our Two-Party System Natural?" *Annals, American Academy of Political and Social Science*, vol. 209 (1948), pp. 1–9.

6. Judson L. James, *American Political Parties* (Pegasus, 1969), p. 45.

7. William H. Riker, *The Theory of Political Coalitions* (Yale University Press, 1962).

8. The influence of the single-member district is strong throughout western democracies. See Douglas W. Rae, *The Political Consequences of Electoral Laws* (Yale University Press, 1967), chap. 5.

9. See Donald V. Smiley, "The Two Party Systems and One-party Dominance in the Liberal Democratic State," *Canadian Journal of Economics and Political Science*, vol. 24 (August 1958), pp. 312–22.

10. Gerald M. Pomper, *Elections in America: Control and Influence in Democratic Politics* (Dodd, Mead, 1968), p. 48.

The strength of the two major parties is bolstered by partisan loyalties; strong partisans support the candidate of their party despite the appeal of other candidates.[11] A new party invariably finds it difficult to overcome well-established voting habits. Politicians also gravitate toward the major parties since they are the only effective channel to office and patronage; third parties must therefore depend on other resources for organizational strength.

Direct party primaries also serve to maintain the dominance of the major parties. Primaries allow for the expression of dissent and popular challenges to reigning party leaders through intraparty elections. Thus, whereas internal conflicts and disenchantment often led to third-party movements at the local and state, and occasionally at national, levels in the nineteenth century, the primary system now offers dissident groups a means of resolving their differences within the confines of their party. Leaders may change, but ideally all factions will remain united in opposition to the common enemy: the other major party. As George McGovern demonstrated in 1972, even presidential nominations can be heavily influenced through concerted primary efforts. And as the 1972 election demonstrated, there is no guarantee that all those who vote on the losing side in a primary will support the party nominee on election day.

The position of the major parties is reinforced by a myriad of statutory barriers to third parties—complex ballot laws, petition requirements, filing deadlines, and limited access to broadcasting. These statutory barriers discourage third parties from entering competition, while such constitutional provisions as a single chief executive and single-member districts encourage a two-party system.

Third parties, in short, rarely provide serious competition for the two major parties in American presidential elections. Yet third parties persist. This book examines the conditions that allow for the rise of third parties and their impact on the outcome of elec-

11. William H. Flanigan, *Political Behavior of the American Electorate* (Allyn and Bacon, 1968), p. 36.

tions and on public policy. Finally, it weighs the case for third parties in a two-party system.

## Identifying Significant Third Parties

Despite the strong tendencies toward two-party competition, dozens of third parties have entered presidential elections. One or more of these contenders has received at least 1 percent of the popular vote in almost two-thirds of the elections since 1828, when the party system assumed its contemporary form,[12] yet there has been no serious breach in the two-party pattern. Third parties rarely receive much attention; they do become widely noticed when they cut deeply into the constituencies of the traditional major parties, as George Wallace did in 1968.

If the criterion of voter appeal is established as the measure of third-party success, the significant contenders can be simply and unambiguously identified. The significant third parties listed in Table 1-1 are those that received a greater number of votes than the average number received by all third-party participants in presidential elections between 1828 and 1972.[13] The average third-party vote cast for the presidency equaled 5.6 percent of the total popular vote. Ten parties have surpassed that average in eight elections; they extend from the Anti-Mason party of 1832 to the American Independent party of 1968.

12. Richard P. McCormick, *The Second American Party System: Party Formation in the Jacksonian Era* (University of North Carolina Press, 1966), chap. 7; and Edgar E. Robinson, *The Evolution of American Political Parties* (Harcourt, Brace, 1924), chap. 7.

13. This criterion for identifying significant third parties is suggested by William Nisbet Chambers, "The Two-Party Norm in American Politics: Will It Survive?" (paper prepared for delivery at the 1968 annual meeting of the American Historical Association), pp. 4–6. Chambers's test has certain drawbacks. It excludes parties that show signs of becoming significant but are effectively countered by the major parties prior to an election—the Progressives of Henry A. Wallace and the southern-based States' Rights party of J. Strom Thurmond, for instance, each won only 2.4 percent of the popular vote in 1948. It also excludes parties with long histories of participation in presidential campaigns; the Prohibition party, for example, has entered presidential contenders since its inception in 1872, never receiving more than 2.3 percent of the popular vote; the Socialist Labor party has fielded presidential contenders since the late nineteenth century without winning more than a fraction of 1 percent of the vote.

TABLE 1-1. *Significant Third Parties in Presidential Elections, 1828–1972*

| Year | Party | Percentage of total votes cast |
|------|-------|-------------------------------|
| 1832 | Anti-Mason | 8.0 |
| 1848 | Free Soil | 10.1 |
| 1856 | American | 21.4 |
| 1860 | Breckinridge Democratic | 18.2 |
|      | Constitutional Union | 12.6 |
| 1892 | Populist | 8.5 |
| 1912 | Theodore Roosevelt Progressive[a] | 27.4 |
|      | Socialist | 6.0 |
| 1924 | La Follette Progressive | 16.6 |
| 1968 | American Independent | 13.5 |

Sources: U.S. Bureau of the Census, *Historical Statistics of the United States, Colonial Times to 1957* (1960), Table Y 27–31; Congressional Quarterly Service, *Politics in America* (3rd ed., Congressional Quarterly Service, 1969), pp. 124–27; and Svend Petersen, ed., *A Statistical History of American Presidential Elections* (Frederick Ungar, 1963).

a. The vote for the Republican party was 23.2 percent, making the vote of the short-lived Progressive party the second highest of the election.

## The American Independent Party

The only third party to qualify as "significant" in the last forty years—the American Independent party (AIP)—won 13.5 percent of the total popular vote in the 1968 election. During the preceding three years, as concern and controversy mounted over the fundamental issues of race and war, an alienated minority became increasingly susceptible to the appeals of a third party.

### POLITICS OF CRISIS

By 1968 the leading domestic concerns of the American electorate had shifted from a variety of personal economic problems and a desire for improved education, prevalent in the late 1950s and early 1960s, to a preoccupation with race relations. Passive acceptance of the civil rights movement of the early 1960s gave way to apprehension and fear after the urban riots in New York's Harlem in 1964 and Los Angeles's Watts in 1965. As riots, looting, and violent deaths increased, militancy grew on all sides. Race affected almost every public issue.

"What do you think is the *most* important problem facing the country today?"[14] In 1960 the general threat of war and concern about foreign relations were the answers most often given to the Gallup survey question.[15] The leading domestic issue cited was economic problems—inflation and higher prices—which were of concern to 12 percent of those polled; racial and educational problems were cited, but less often. When the question was posed again, four years later, concerns had changed appreciably. After the first major urban riots of the decade, in July 1964, the "racial issue" was the most important problem for 61 percent of the public.[16] Preoccupation with civil rights and race relations continued throughout the next four years, giving way only to the even more provocative issue of Vietnam. In 1968 the responses changed from civil rights and urban unrest to "law and order" and urban unrest, but the underlying racial dimension remained unchanged. On the eve of the election, the Survey Research Center of the University of Michigan found that 28 percent of the voters saw "racial and public order" as the leading national issue.[17] The carryover into the electoral arena was unavoidable. As an election issue, race relations was not very important in the presidential campaign of 1960, but it had grown in importance by 1964, and in 1968 it was central.

As the domestic debate over race raged, U.S. foreign policy in Southeast Asia became an even more divisive issue. By 1968, Vietnam stood for controversy, conflict, protest, indeed national crisis. In some quarters there was moral opposition to having the United States involved in a foreign war; in others disagreement with the method of involvement, either as half-hearted or as over-commit-

14. Information on the leading issues of public concern in the United States is drawn from response to this question, repeated over the years by the American Institute of Public Opinion (the Gallup organization).

15. V. O. Key, Jr., *The Responsible Electorate* (Belknap Press of Harvard University Press, 1966), p. 131.

16. Press release, American Institute of Public Opinion, Aug. 21, 1964.

17. Response to the question: "As you well know, the government faces many serious problems in this country and in other parts of the world. What do you personally feel are the most important problems the government in Washington should try to take care of?" "The Survey Research Center 1968 American National Election Study" (Ann Arbor: Inter-University Consortium for Political Research, 1971; processed).

ment; elsewhere a fear of the loss of national prestige; and most often the realization that Vietnam was severely dividing the nation.

National preoccupation with the war developed in the short span of one year. Before the Tonkin Resolution of August 1964, only 7 percent of the electorate considered the Vietnam situation of primary concern, but by August 1965, Vietnam had become the dominant issue in the nation.[18] With slight variation from one month to the next, the issue remained dominant through 1968. The great influence of Vietnam on concern about international affairs is apparent in Figure 1-1.

Thus, as election day 1968 approached, Vietnam and race relations were clearly the two most important and frustrating issues facing the nation.

A NATION DIVIDED

Crisis was crucial to the AIP vote. Equally important was the division within the electorate, which created a minority estranged from both major parties. The early response to the war was one of "inattentive tolerance towards the U.S. Government's actions in South Vietnam."[19] By the presidential campaign of 1968 this attitude had drastically altered. The U.S. commitment of troops had mushroomed to 530,000 and the country had sustained over 30,000 casualties; more and more signs indicated that the war would be a protracted and costly venture, with little hope of ultimate success.

While a majority of Americans considered themselves "hawks" on Vietnam in late 1967, a majority of both Republicans and Democrats favored turning the war over completely to the South Vietnamese by stages—Vietnamization—or turning the entire problem over to the United Nations. The other alternatives offered in the October Gallup survey—continuation of the existing policy of gradual escalation; turning over the entire direction of the war to the military; immediate withdrawal; and de-escalation and a cessa-

18. *Gallup Opinion Index*, December 1967, pp. 9 and 16.
19. Philip E. Converse and Howard Schuman, " 'Silent Majorities' and the Vietnam War," *Scientific American*, vol. 222 (June 1970), p. 19.

FIGURE I-I. *Public Concern about the War in Vietnam,*
*August 1964 to March 1969*[a]

Leading concern, percent of all responses

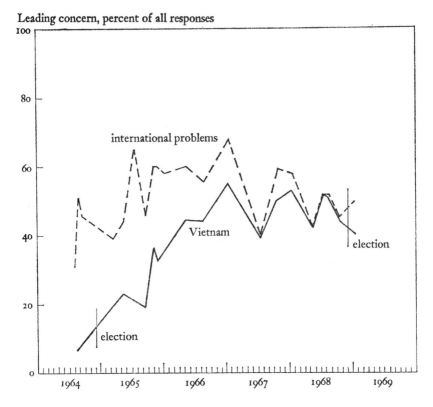

Sources: *Gallup Opinion Index*, monthly issues, 1964–68; and George Gallup,
*The Gallup Poll: Public Opinion 1935–1971*, vol. 3 (Random House, 1972).
a. Vietnam figures from mid-1966 to mid-1967 are approximations.

tion of bombing—received less than majority support. Meanwhile,
20 percent of the public continued to seek "all out victory."[20]

As the controversy grew between those morally outraged at the
actions of the United States, those opposing the war on more pragmatic grounds, and those favoring the war, the national attitude
steadily shifted in one direction: against the war. A key impetus
was the surprising military prowess the North Vietnamese had

20. *Gallup Opinion Index*, December 1967, p. 38.

shown in their Tet offensive of February 1968. Following Tet, more and more Americans lost confidence in the war effort as well as in the government's persistently optimistic forecasts of imminent victory. The changing public mood is clearly reflected in the change in the proportion of self-identified hawks: from 61 percent of a sample of the voting population in February 1968 to only 41 percent a month later.[21] Peace sentiment grew apace; "dove" self-identification increased in the same period from 23 percent to 42 percent of those surveyed.[22] While there may have been confusion over who opposed the war on which grounds—moral, pragmatic, or any other—the trend was obvious.[23]

The divisions over Vietnam in early 1968 altered little throughout the presidential campaign. In July 1968, 66 percent of Gallup's interviewees stated they would vote for a candidate proposing a de-escalation of American forces, while 18 percent would not.[24] There was a slight shift toward the withdrawal position in the months immediately preceding the election.[25] By election day the overriding demarcation in the electorate was between a minority tenaciously committed to achieving a military victory and a majority that sought withdrawal.

The latter group was itself split between advocates of immediate withdrawal and more gradual de-escalation or Vietnamization. This division, however, was one of degree, not of kind. A candidate could equivocate in this area, calling for withdrawal as soon as possible, or immediately, without alienating either faction. It would have been far more difficult for a candidate to attempt to bridge the gap between the withdrawal and military-victory positions.

21. Ibid., May 1968, p. 20.
22. Ibid.
23. Converse and Schuman, "Silent Majorities," note the steady growth of the withdrawal position and conclude that most of the disenchantment with the war was pragmatic; the United States was losing and showed little prospect of doing otherwise.
24. *Gallup Opinion Index*, August 1968, p. 17.
25. Richard A. Brody and others, "Vietnam, the Urban Crisis, and the 1968 Presidential Election: A Preliminary Analysis" (paper prepared for delivery at the September 1969 meeting of the American Sociological Association in San Francisco; processed).

The racial divisions, while somewhat more complex, followed a similar pattern. The sharp division in attitudes toward racial segregation was between those willing to negotiate over the appropriate pace and degree of integration and those opposed to integration in any form. By 1968 the vast majority of the public had concluded segregation could no longer be accepted as public policy. Only 15 percent of the respondents to one survey remained in favor of segregation—one-third fewer than in 1964. Meanwhile, 35 percent placed themselves in favor of integration and the remaining 45 percent sought some middle ground.[26]

Although it is unclear what "some middle ground" meant, it does convey the notion that some accommodation with blacks was acceptable. For the segregationists, however, there seemed to be no room for compromise; anything short of maintaining the traditional pattern of segregation would set the country on an irreversible course, and everything would thus be lost. Consequently, the crucial split over race relations in 1968 was between the segregationists on one end of the spectrum and the remainder of the population on the other.

A less explicit indicator of racial attitude is found in the reaction to urban unrest, a euphemism for riots, robbery, and disorder in the black urban communities. In a national survey in November of 1968 on solutions to the problem of urban unrest, 23 percent of the respondents chose a solution calling for "solving the problems of poverty and unemployment." In sharp contrast, 20 percent identified the "use of all available force" as the appropriate solution. The remaining 57 percent fell into five positions between these two extremes.[27]

These responses to the urban unrest issue reveal two sizable minorities, with the bulk of the electorate adhering to a centrist position. In ordinary election years this distribution would be likely to produce a typical two-party split, with each of the traditional

26. Responses in 1964 and 1968 to the question: "What about you. Are you in favor of desegregation, strict segregation, or something in between?" Survey Research Center, Election Studies for 1964 (rev. ed., 1971) and 1968.

27. Responses on a seven-point self-ranking scale. Brody and others, "Vietnam, the Urban Crisis, and the 1968 Presidential Election."

parties seeking the center while making only guarded appeals to one of the extremes. However, the disquiet over urban unrest was often tied to anxieties over race relations and became important to the AIP effort. Gallup found that by 1968 "Wallace supporters tend[ed] to be 'hawks' not only on Vietnam but on domestic issues as well."[28] It appears that the overlapping of the minority views among Wallace supporters on the two highly controversial issues added to the intensity of the split between the majority and the minority.

CANDIDATES AND THEIR POSITIONS

The presence of the intense minority became important to Wallace and the AIP because the minority views were not represented by the major parties. In 1968 neither Richard Nixon nor Hubert Humphrey actively appealed to the hawk position on the war or the segregationist position on race. That both candidates would not do so is understandable. For Nixon, the standard-bearer of the party out of power, adopting the most popular position on Vietnam would be an obvious strategy. His message on the war was at the same time highly ambiguous and very much to the point; he had a "plan for peace," one that would bring the war to an honorable conclusion while bringing American boys home. Humphrey's strategic considerations were also fairly well defined. If he were to disassociate himself from the Johnson administration and carry the highly vocal antiwar faction of the Democratic party, he would have to repudiate the administration line and become an advocate of withdrawal, an approach he ultimately took.

On race relations, Nixon and Humphrey held different positions, but neither provided much solace to the segregationists. Humphrey throughout his career in public office had been a leader of those advocating strong federal action to end segregation. His name became synonymous with civil rights when he led the battle over that platform plank at the 1948 Democratic convention. Thus

28. This overlap was particularly prevalent in 1968 among Wallace voters; see George Gallup, Jr., and John O. Davies III, "The Mood of the Electorate—An In-Depth Report," *Gallup Opinion Index*, October 1968, pp. 2–4.

while other Democrats might have tried to skirt the active-federal-intervention position on integration associated with the Democratic party in 1968—hoping to broaden the party's appeal among white voters—Humphrey did not, and probably could not have even if he had so desired.

Nixon was more of an unknown quantity. He was opposed to segregation but also to the demonstrations and violence and the active role of the federal government that the public associated with the civil rights and desegregation movement. In this sense he reflected the view of white "middle America." As early as 1964 he had articulated a dual strategy for satisfying both the moral and the private choices of the majority of the white population, condemning segregation but rejecting federal action: "We oppose segregation in our schools either by law or in fact. But this problem must be dealt with in an orderly transition. We believe it is detrimental to both Negro and white children to uproot them from their communities and to haul them from one school to another in order to force integration in an artificial and unworkable manner."[29] By 1968 new civil rights laws had been added to the statute books, but Nixon maintained his dual position. As a candidate, he stated: "I oppose any action by the Office of Education that goes beyond a mandate of Congress; a case in point is the busing of students to achieve racial balance in schools. The law clearly states that 'desegregation shall not mean the assignment of students to public schools in order to overcome racial imbalance.' "[30]

Long before it became clear that Nixon and Humphrey would relinquish the field on the hawk and segregationist positions, the AIP existed in embryo. George Wallace, the man who vowed never to be "out-nigguhed again" upon losing to the irreconcilable segregationist John Patterson in the 1958 Alabama gubernatorial race;[31] who when inaugurated as governor in 1963 declared from the steps of the state capitol, "segregation now . . . segregation

---

29. From a Lincoln's birthday speech in Cincinnati, quoted in Stephen Hess and David S. Broder, *The Republican Establishment: The Present and Future of the G.O.P.* (Harper and Row, 1967), p. 168.

30. *Nixon on the Issues* (Nixon-Agnew Campaign Committee, 1968), p. 98.

31. Marshal Frady, *Wallace* (Meridian, 1970), pp. 125–27.

tomorrow . . . segregation forever"; and who six months later at-tempted to bar the entrance into the University of Alabama of its first two black students in defiance of federal desegregation orders, was laying the groundwork for his presidential bid well in advance of the 1968 election.

With the growing discontent of whites both North and South, the acceleration in integration being sought by the courts and the federal government, and the army of civil rights activists invading the South in the early 1960s, Wallace entered the 1964 presidential contest. He did not expect to win a majority of popular votes but did anticipate winning enough electoral votes to throw the election into the House of Representatives, where he could demand impor-tant concessions on civil rights. Despite his showing in the Demo-cratic primaries of Wisconsin, Indiana, and Maryland in the spring, where he received 34 percent, 32 percent, and 43 percent of the votes, respectively,[32] his campaign was short-lived. Wallace's plan first faltered when his supporters failed to place Wallace-pledged electors on the Mississippi, Georgia, and South Carolina ballots. The final blow was the Republican party's nomination of Senator Barry Goldwater, one of the leading conservatives in the nation and a man who had just voted against the Civil Rights Act. Four days later Wallace withdrew from the contest, claiming to have accomplished his ultimate goal of "conservatizing both major parties."

Wallace apparently failed in his effort to conservatize the na-tional parties in 1964. Under the Johnson administration the Voting Rights acts were adopted; Martin Luther King, Jr., journeyed to Selma, Alabama, Wallace's home territory, to dramatize the bars to Negro voting in southern states; and the federal government and the courts continued to press for desegregation. Meanwhile, the Goldwater forces were replaced by the moderates within the Re-publican national organization.

Wallace reacted in turn. As the key campaigner for his wife's bid for the governorship of Alabama in 1966 (under state law,

32. Michael Rogin, "Wallace and the Middle Class: The White Backlash in Wisconsin," *Public Opinion Quarterly*, vol. 30 (Spring 1966), p. 98.

Wallace could not succeed himself in office), Wallace promised that if the major parties "ran the folks they're talking about now," he would be ready to take up the challenge again as a presidential candidate in 1968.

Wallace could not in 1967 have predicted President Johnson's premature retirement from politics, ensuring that the Democratic party would fall into the hands of one or the other of the party's leading civil rights protagonists, Hubert Humphrey and Robert Kennedy. Added to this, "the death of his old adversary, Martin Luther King, came like a miracle. The riots King's murder touched off meant that the 1968 campaign would be fought on Wallace's chosen ground. The theme would be his theme: law and order."[33]

Prior to these momentous events, it appeared that Wallace had strong reservations about the fruitfulness of an all-out third-party campaign. Instead, he sought influence and recognition without risking a potentially abortive independent race for the presidency. As in 1964, he apparently hoped to carry a sufficient number of southern states to hold the balance of power in the electoral college. In February 1968, for example, Wallace revealed his conditions for forming a coalition with one of the major-party candidates: he would throw his electoral votes to the candidate who promised, among other things, to "punish treason" by putting Vietnam dissenters in jail, to eliminate the federal antipoverty program, to abandon any type of civil rights legislation, and to return to the states control over school and hospital integration, open housing legislation, reapportionment, and congressional redistricting.[34] In this first attempt at a presidential campaign, experience in organizing in each state and national recognition would be gained; the serious bid for victory would be reserved for 1972. Only after the disastrous Democratic convention of 1968 and Wallace's appreciable gain in the opinion polls in mid-summer—up to 22 per-

33. Lewis Chester, Godfrey Hodgson, and Bruce Page, *An American Melodrama: The Presidential Campaign of 1968* (Dell, 1969), p. 290.

34. "The Public Record of George C. Wallace," *Congressional Quarterly Weekly Report*, vol. 26 (Sept. 27, 1968), p. 11.

cent—did he actually believe he could win in 1968 and attempt to do so.[35]

Clearly, then, Wallace was in the field as early as 1964 and may have had serious intentions of building a third-party movement for 1972. The nucleus of his party organization was very much in existence, awaiting the proper moment to enter the electoral arena. The crisis over race relations was Wallace's key issue, but the significant third-party bid of 1968 could only have been launched with the additional crisis over Vietnam, and, of utmost importance, the rejection of the segregationist and hawk positions by Nixon and Humphrey.

Despite the distortions and misperceptions introduced in communications between candidates and voters, the public was able to identify the positions of the three leading candidates on the principal issues of 1968. In general, the electorate saw Nixon and Humphrey as equivocating but basically agreeing on Vietnam. Typically, major-party candidates attempt to be on the majority side of key issues and yet not alienate the subgroups constituting the majority. In their public addresses both Nixon and Humphrey gave mixed signals, but most of them pointed to withdrawal.[36] In effect, this stand placed the two candidates on one side of the controversy over Vietnam, leaving the military-victory adherents without a major-party advocate.

Differences between the major-party candidates in their positions on urban unrest were more clearly perceived by the public. While both Nixon and Humphrey were seen as equivocating across a scale of alternatives that ran from "solve problems of poverty and unemployment" to "use all available force," Humphrey was identified more with the "solve problems" end of the spectrum—toward the left.[37] Nixon was very much in the center.

---

35. Forrest Harrell Armstrong, "George C. Wallace: Insurgent on the Right" (Ph.D. thesis, University of Michigan, 1970), pp. 10–11.

36. Benjamin I. Page and Richard A. Brody, "Policy Voting and the Electoral Process: The Vietnam War Issue," *American Political Science Review*, vol. 66 (September 1972), especially pp. 983–86.

37. Brody and others, "Vietnam, the Urban Crisis, and the 1968 Presidential Election," table 7, p. 16a.

Wallace, on the other hand, was identified with the hard-line position on urban unrest. This and his extreme military-victory position on Vietnam were consistent with Wallace's record as a segregationist, with his continued denunciation of "soft" treatment of urban rioters and protesters, and with his nomination of General Curtis E. LeMay, an advocate of unrestrained military power, as his running mate on the 1968 AIP ticket. In contrast to the extreme positions taken by Wallace, the major-party candidates despite their differences were viewed by the electorate as quite unsympathetic to these minority views.

THE 1968 VOTE

The significant third-party vote in 1968 occurred in a period of clear political crisis, of intense minority interest in two issues (and a coincidence of the dissenting groups), and of little sympathy from the major parties for the minority positions. The Wallace organization was able to capitalize on these circumstances and mount an effective challenge to the major parties.

Common sense suggests that the large vote accorded Wallace came from the intense minority and was a result of his stand on issues. Yet students of voting behavior have often noted the errors of assuming that voters uniformly perceive candidates as representing clearly defined positions or that they vote on the basis of the policy positions of candidates.[38] Also, if the candidates' positions on controversial issues are not distinctive, voters can hardly express their preferences on the issues.[39] They must either make a random choice or fall back on such traditional inducements as party label.

The electorate in 1968 might well be expected to have exhibited a high level of issue voting. With only a few very controversial

38. See Angus Campbell and others, *The American Voter* (Wiley, 1969), chap. 8; David E. RePass, "Issue Salience and Party Choice," *American Political Science Review*, vol. 65 (June 1971), p. 400; and Gerald M. Pomper, "From Confusion to Clarity: Issues and American Voters, 1956–1968," Richard W. Boyd, "Popular Control of Public Policy: A Normal Vote Analysis of the 1968 Election," and comments of Richard A. Brody and Benjamin I. Page and of John H. Kessel, in *American Political Science Review*, vol. 66 (June 1972), pp. 415–65.

39. Page and Brody, "Policy Voting and the Electoral Process," p. 980.

issues before the public, and with a new party in the field that could not rely on traditional party ties, voters could be expected to be aware of candidate positions and to have voted their policy preferences.

Since the public perceptions of Nixon and Humphrey on the leading controversial issue, Vietnam, were almost identical, it is not surprising that only 2 percent of the electorate appear to have chosen between the two men on the basis of this issue.[40] The dimensions that most distinguished Humphrey from Nixon in the eyes of the electorate, and proved to be the best indicators of voting for each of them, were those of traditional party identification and attitudes toward governmental social welfare activities.[41]

In contrast, the best indicator of voting for Wallace was the voters' attitudes on the racial issue—civil rights and law and order —followed by their views on Vietnam, the cold war, social welfare, and the role of the federal government. While the predictive value of these indicators was stronger in the South than elsewhere, it varied only slightly across the nation.[42]

Not only were the Wallace voters issue oriented; they also held the minority position on the issues and were passionate in their convictions. On the key question of racial integration, the Survey Research Center found that 40 percent of the Wallace supporters, all of whom were white, desired segregation, in contrast to only 10 percent of the white voters of the two major parties.[43] Furthermore, over half of the Wallace supporters took extreme stands on urban unrest, and 86 percent of those taking extreme positions advocated the use of all available force as the solution to the prob-

40. Ibid., p. 982.

41. Herbert F. Weisberg and Jerrold G. Rusk, "Dimensions of Candidate Evaluation," *American Political Science Review*, vol. 64 (December 1970), p. 1178.

42. Philip E. Converse and others, "Continuity and Change in American Politics: Parties and Issues in the 1968 Election," *American Political Science Review*, vol. 63 (December 1969), pp. 1097–98. See also Seymour Martin Lipset and Earl Raab, "The Wallace Whitelash," *Trans-action*, vol. 7 (December 1969), pp. 23–35; and Arthur G. Wolfe, "Challenge from the Right: The Basis of Voter Support for Wallace in 1968" (paper prepared for delivery at the 1969 annual meeting of the American Psychological Association), pp. 1–20.

43. Converse and others, "Continuity and Change in American Politics," p. 1097.

lem.[44] Similarly on Vietnam, of the almost two-thirds of the Wallace supporters taking an extreme stand, 83 percent sought a complete military victory. Of those in the Wallace camp with extreme feelings on both issues, 77 percent jointly responded "use force" on the urban and "complete victory" on the Vietnam question, while only 2 percent held the opposing views. The issue-oriented segments of the major parties were not so close to unanimity on the solution to these problems.[45]

Most of the Wallace voters were overwhelmingly committed to the minority positions on race relations and the war. Yet issue-oriented voters may unintentionally vote for an equivocating candidate who is not really closest to their policy preferences. Often partisan ties keep dissidents loyal in spite of disagreements on policy. And to some extent voters project their own view on the candidate of their choice, without reference to his policy positions. Therefore, even in the face of the fervent Wallace appeal, many "hawks" and "hard liners" as well as some segregationists gave their votes to Nixon or Humphrey. A third party cannot anticipate the support of every member of the intense minority whose views it champions. Nevertheless, sufficient numbers of the estranged minority do vote their policy preferences to make a successful third party possible.

Third-party voters in 1968 were alike in a number of other ways. As a group they had received less formal education, were younger, and had less confidence in the operations of the government and political institutions than other voters, and they were disproportionately male, often with a rural, southern background.[46] Wallace voters saw themselves, when compared with other groups

44. "Extreme" represents the last and next-to-last positions at either end of the 1968 Survey Research Center urban unrest and Vietnam scales. The intensity of opinions is greatest at the extreme ends of issue scales. See V. O. Key, Jr., *Public Opinion and American Democracy* (Knopf, 1961), chap. 9.

45. Among Republicans holding extreme views, almost equal numbers were at the two poles. Among Democrats, over one-half held the "solve problems" and "withdrawal" positions.

46. James McEvoy III, *Radicals or Conservatives? The Contemporary American Right* (Rand McNally, 1971), pp. 141–45.

in the society, as deprived of their share of America's wealth.[47] Support of the AIP candidate can also be explained as an expression of interacting racial and ethnic sentiments.[48] But these socio-economic and psychological factors exist almost constantly from one election to the next. Thus, they do not adequately explain why significant third-party voting develops, as it does, in only a limited number of elections.

## Two-Party versus Three-Party Elections

The conditions under which third parties can be expected to do well are revealed by a comparison of the 1968 election with the two-party contests of 1960, 1964, and 1972. Over the period of the four elections the factors that encourage the formation of two competing major parties, such as the need for alliances in the contest for the presidency and single-member districts, remained unchanged. Thus, institutional factors provide few clues as to why a significant third party appeared in 1968.

### THE 1960 ELECTION

In 1960 no single issue, or set of issues, was paramount, an obvious dissimilarity between the 1960 and 1968 elections. Many limited concerns were of interest to various groups in 1960; the outstanding issue was the threat of war in general, cited by 18 percent of those polled by Gallup; foreign relations, communicating, understanding, and getting along with other people and nations were also cited by 18 percent. Other lesser concerns were domestic economic problems, inflation, higher prices, unemployment, U.S. relations with the Soviet Union and Cuba, race relations, and education.[49]

---

47. Thomas F. Pettigrew, Robert T. Riley, and Reeve D. Vanneman, "George Wallace's Constituents," *Psychology Today*, vol. 5 (February 1972).

48. Walter Dean Burnham and John Sprague, "Additive and Multiplicative Models of the Voting Universe: The Case of Pennsylvania: 1960–1968," *American Political Science Review*, vol. 64 (June 1970), pp. 471–90.

49. Key, *Responsible Electorate*, pp. 130–31.

The spread of issues in 1960 closely approximates that of the ideal two-party system. The many issues seemed to affirm that the diversity of peoples, regions, religions, education, and economic levels throughout the nation results in political parties that are aggregations of interests, not distinct representatives of any single segment of the society. Although some interests may be found more often represented in one of the parties, all major segments are sufficiently represented in each to inhibit exclusion of any segment from government decision making, no matter which party is in power. Because of the diversity of concerns, candidates win elections by accumulating support from a wide variety of groups. The winning vote, in such instances, is not considered a mandate for action on a single overriding issue so much as a mandate to take marginal steps in many directions. Through this process it is assumed that all factions will eventually be satisfied by the government as power shifts between the major parties. Politics is a low-key scuffle over limited and short-run advantages.

In elections with many rather than a few exceptionally important issues, third-party candidates have rarely been able to arouse a large following by contrasting themselves to both of the major parties. If they concentrate on only one or two issues in a multiple-issue election, they cannot expect to gain a significant national following. Yet if they seek a broader base by addressing a multiplicity of issues, they become caught up in the cross-pressures and compromising positions characteristic of major-party candidates. But who will vote for a new party when it provides little more than the old ones and has far less chance of victory? Not surprisingly, no third party has prospered under these conditions.

### THE 1964 ELECTION

It takes more than a few highly controversial issues for a third party to do well. Under certain circumstances the two major parties are able to contain warring factions. In 1964 a few issues sharply divided the country. But the two major parties divided on either side of the conflict, effectively preventing a successful third-party vote.

The paramount domestic issues were neither new nor unmanageable within the traditional Republican and Democratic framework. The election provided a contest between candidates representing the "conservative" and "liberal" positions as generally defined in the post-New Deal era. The conservative credentials of the Republican nominee, Barry Goldwater, were impeccable. Throughout his career Goldwater had called for lower taxes, more efficiency in government, a reversal of growing federal powers, and the elimination of social security. On grounds of personal liberties, furthermore, he had voted against the Civil Rights Act of 1964. Goldwater claimed that he offered the American electorate their first real opportunity to affirm or reject the New Deal domestic policies—a choice, not an echo, of liberal positions.

Lyndon Johnson, the incumbent Democratic nominee, represented a renewed commitment to the welfare state policies of the New Deal. Johnson did not employ the rhetoric of liberalism, but he espoused liberal programs, notably federal civil rights laws and a "war" against domestic poverty.

Because of the encompassing nature of the Goldwater-Johnson competition, there remained little leeway for any third party to establish a distinctive position on the leading issues. Thus George Wallace, the most potent third-party contender, withdrew following the nomination of Goldwater, whose views were close to his own.

### THE 1972 ELECTION

The positions advocated by the major parties in 1972, as well as the shift in public sentiments between 1968 and 1972, brought about the demise of the AIP, just four years following its appreciable electoral appeal. Leading administration officials in the first Nixon administration, including Attorney General John N. Mitchell, Vice President Spiro T. Agnew, and the President, all catered to the apprehension about law and order exploited so effectively by George Wallace in 1968. Using the rhetoric of the third-party contender, the administration provided the 1972 voter sensitive to the law-and-order and racial issue a choice between itself and a third party unlikely to win. Moreover, the public perceived a slow-down in the movement toward integration with the Republican administration that took office in 1969.[50] Although Wallace was viewed as more prone to use police power in attaining law and order and more committed to undoing integration than either of the major parties, the Republican party went a long way toward undermining the third-party appeal on these issues.

The sharp decline in ghetto riots and student antiwar protests between 1969 and 1972 also worked against the AIP. Without these visible provocations, Wallace or any other AIP candidate would be hard pressed in 1972 to stir much reaction against the "establishment" on these issues. In addition, in the three years following the 1968 campaign the public lost confidence in Wallace as the appropriate man to deal with the problems he had been so closely identified with. The proportion of people who believed Wallace "would keep law and order the way it should be kept" declined by almost one-third over the period—from 43 percent in a 1968 survey to 28 percent in a 1971 survey.[51] Many 1968 Wallace partisans had reconsidered their choice by 1971, not because they disagreed with the positions of the candidate, but because they felt the need for a more conciliatory leader than they expected Wallace would be.[52] This suggests a general desire for a cooling off and a negative reaction to the combative controversy of 1968. The diffuse public discontent in 1972 was not nearly as emotional or aggressive as in 1968. Before Wallace had to abandon his campaign, one canvasser had concluded that 50 percent of the Alabama's city voters of 1968 would shift either to Nixon or the Democratic nominee in the 1972 general election.[53]

50. In February 1969, 48 percent of those surveyed by Gallup predicted that under the Nixon administration integration would be pushed "not so fast," 28 percent "about right," and 16 percent "faster." *Gallup Opinion Index*, March 1969, p. 2.

51. Louis Harris, "Is George Wallace Losing His Political Grip?" *Chicago Tribune*, Oct. 21, 1971.

52. Based on a poll by David Broder and Haynes Johnson of 300 prospective 1972 voters in eight states, reported in "Wallace, Agnew Views Trouble Even Partisans," *Washington Post*, Dec. 15, 1971.

53. Samuel Lubell, "Old Wallace Voters Key?" *Washington Evening Star*, April 18, 1972.

Even with the continuing divisiveness over school busing, Wallace was losing support in his basic constituency. His support in the deep South declined by 24 percentage points between 1968 and 1971, from 54 percent to 30 percent,[54] and this was the area where a campaign aimed at accumulating electoral college votes in 1972 would have had to be concentrated. These were warnings to both Wallace and his adversaries that he probably would not do nearly as well in the states of Alabama, Georgia, Louisiana, and Mississippi, which he had carried in the general election in 1968. Also pertinent in the South of 1972 were the shifting attitudes of the newly elected state leaders in the region, both Democratic and Republican, who avoided volatile confrontations over racial issues. This trend was reflected in the moderate positions taken by the governors of Virginia, South Carolina, Florida, Georgia, Tennessee, and Arkansas, who publicly called for accommodations between the races and rejected the flamboyant campaign styles and racial attacks characteristic of Wallace and old-style southern politicians.[55]

Still, Wallace might have based his entry as a third-party candidate in 1972 on his original following, on new support based on 1972 issues, or on both. Concern about economic issues had developed across the nation between the 1968 and 1972 elections,[56] and Wallace gained attention with an attack on inequalities in the tax structure. He also raised the issue of military power—whether the United States would remain foremost among nations. However, Wallace could not offer an alternative in 1972 as distinct as in 1968 on the issues of tax inequalities, a "first strike capacity" for the United States, or busing. President Nixon joined in arguing the need for military superiority, and both Nixon and McGovern called for changes in the tax structure.

54. Harris, "Is George Wallace Losing His Political Grip?"

55. Earl Black, "Southern Governors and Political Change: Campaign Stances on Racial Segregation and Economic Development, 1950–69," *Journal of Politics*, vol. 33 (August 1971), pp. 703–34.

56. In the Gallup survey of late August 1971, 45 percent of the responders identified "economic problems" as the most important problem facing the country, 25 percent "Vietnam," 12 percent "crime and lawlessness," and 7 percent "race relations." *Gallup Opinion Index*, October 1971. In November "state of economy" was identi-

On the issue of school busing to attain integration the picture was less clear. President Nixon had rejected any policy of busing to achieve racially balanced schools, while most of the Democratic candidates for President had moderated their tone, conceding busing as one of the necessary tools of achieving equality in education. The important unknown was the public perception of each candidate. No matter what the Republican and Democratic candidates said, the electorate might have refused to believe that they seriously intended to prevent school integration, whereas Wallace's promise could be taken seriously.[57] Thus, if schools had opened in 1972 with the massive opposition to busing and outbreaks of violence that had occurred in Pontiac, Michigan, in 1971, and if Wallace was seen as the only candidate seriously opposing busing, then his support could have been expected to grow. But Nixon's disassociation from the court-ordered implementation of busing programs made his claim of opposition to busing plausible too. Even though Wallace criticized the President for not being sufficiently aggressive, he did not have the antibusing position to himself.

The configuration of candidates and issues in 1972 was quite different from that of 1968, when Wallace held distinctive positions on the issues of race relations and Vietnam. In the months preceding the 1972 election it became evident that in a three-way contest the AIP candidate would not be as likely to capitalize on discontent as in 1968. Apparently George Wallace was aware of the change and thus chose to abandon the third-party approach and become a contestant in the Democratic presidential primaries in 1972.

Whether his entry into the Democratic primaries was an unequivocal rejection of a third-party strategy cannot be known. The

fied by 41 percent as most important and "international problems," ranking second, by 23 percent, this being composed of "Vietnam," 15 percent, and "other," 8 percent. *Gallup Opinion Index*, December 1971. In October 1968, "Vietnam war" was cited by 44 percent, "crime" (including looting and riots) by 25 percent, and "race relations" by 17 percent. *Gallup Opinion Index*, November 1968.

57. In a poll conducted in Maryland on the day of the state's primary, 82 percent of those surveyed identified Wallace with the single issue of busing to achieve racial balance in schools. See Haynes Johnson, "Wallace Weak in Direct Test," *Washington Post*, May 18, 1972.

attempt on his life in Laurel, Maryland, on May 15, at the peak of his primary campaign, effectively removed Wallace from the contest. Had the bleak picture for the AIP changed, he might have headed a third-party bid for the presidency. In 1912, for instance, Theodore Roosevelt began his campaign as a Republican, winning in eleven of the thirteen primaries he entered. When the Taft forces refused to seat many of his delegates to the Republican national convention, Roosevelt bolted the party to lead the Progressives. In 1972, George Wallace chose to go the primary route within the Democratic party and did remarkably well in key areas outside the South, placing second in Indiana, with 42 percent of the popular vote, and carrying the primaries of Michigan with 51 percent and Maryland with 39 percent of the popular vote. Had the deep ideological and personal split between Wallace and the established Democratic party leaders resulted in a failure to seat his delegates at the national party convention, Wallace might have chosen to go the way of Roosevelt. He could have branded the "liberal establishment" of the national party as hypocrites who talk about grass roots participation but reject the "mandate of the people" when it conflicts with their elitist views. Wallace might have led a number of convention delegates, particularly from the South, out of the Democratic party and drawn off a good portion of the Democratic electorate. In such an event he could have rejuvenated the AIP and led it to a popular vote equaling that of 1968.

In fact, the injuries Wallace sustained prevented his participating actively in the Democratic convention or running as the AIP candidate. The combined effects of the appeals of the major parties to the Wallace constituency and the withdrawal of Wallace from center stage resulted in a negligible 1 percent of the popular vote going to the AIP—renamed American party—candidate, John G. Schmitz, in 1972.[58] This withering away of a significant third party soon after its strong electoral showing is not atypical, however,

58. Schmitz, a Republican and member of the John Birch Society who was defeated in his second-term bid to Congress in the Republican primary in 1972, was nominated after Wallace made clear that he would not accept the nomination. Thomas J. Anderson, of Pigeon Forge, Tennessee, also a member of the John Birch Society, was chosen as his running mate.

despite the fact that most third parties have not been handicapped by the sudden removal of their most prominent figure.

The AIP experience suggests that significant third-party voting occurs in a normally two-party system during a period of national political crisis, that is, when a few issues become highly controversial; when one or more of the issues generates an intense minority; when the major parties ignore or attack—in either case alienate —the minority; and when an individual or group of political entrepreneurs then mobilizes the minority behind a third party. Comparison of the elections from 1960 through 1972 indicates that all of these factors must be present—that they act in a cumulative fashion—to produce a significant third-party vote. Seldom do all the factors appear, moreover, in consecutive elections.

☆

*Chapter Two*

☆

# THE HISTORICAL PATTERN
# OF THIRD-PARTY VOTING

T*HE* LEADING precondition for a significant third-party vote is severe political crisis. Only in times of extraordinary stress do the division of public opinion, the positions taken by the major parties, and the energies of third-party entrepreneurs take on importance. Eight episodes of "intense conflict" from the 1830s to the early 1970s have been identified by Robert A. Dahl; they are very similar to ten episodes of "crisis politics" isolated by William Nisbet Chambers.[1] All ten significant third parties have emerged in these periods (see Table 2-1).

No significant third party has appeared at a time other than one of crisis. And only in periods of crisis following the Civil War and during the Great Depression have third parties failed to appear. If the experience of the 1960s is a guide, the absence of significant third parties except in periods of crisis is due to the normal operations of the two-party system. Their absence in two of these periods is related to the size of the warring factions and the positions adopted by the major parties.

## The Egalitarian Ethic

In many ways the intense conflicts of the late 1820s and early 1830s foreshadowed those of later years. The nullification crisis

1. Robert A. Dahl, ed., *Political Oppositions in Western Democracies* (Yale University Press, 1966), pp. 34–69; and William Nisbet Chambers, "Crisis Politics, USA, 1789–1971" (St. Louis: Washington University, 1972; processed).

TABLE 2-1. *Coincidence of Intense Conflict on Issues and Significant Third-Party Vote in Presidential Elections, 1828–1972*

| Issues in conflict[a] | Third party and election year[b] |
|---|---|
| Egalitarianism | Anti-Mason: 1832 |
| New territories, nativism, and slavery | Free Soil: 1848 |
| | American: 1856 |
| | Breckinridge Democratic: 1860 |
| | Constitutional Union: 1860 |
| Reconstruction | *none* |
| Agrarian protest | Populist: 1892 |
| Corporate regulation and government responsiveness | Theodore Roosevelt Progressive: 1912 |
| | Socialist: 1912 |
| | La Follette Progressive: 1924 |
| Great Depression | *none* |
| Civil rights and Vietnam war | American Independent: 1968 |

a. Dominant issues in periods of intense conflict defined by William Nisbet Chambers, "Crisis Politics, USA, 1789–1971" (St. Louis: Washington University, 1972; processed); and Robert A. Dahl, ed., *Political Oppositions in Western Democracies* (Yale University Press, 1966), pp. 34–69.

b. Year in which third party won at least 5.6 percent of presidential vote.

was brought about by the efforts of South Carolina to circumvent federal tariffs on manufactured goods—and was widely publicized in the Senate debate about the nature of the federal union between Robert Y. Hayne of South Carolina and Daniel Webster of Massachusetts. It raised the recurring issue of a state's right to secede from the Union, an option for dissident states considered realizable by many until its futility was demonstrated in the Civil War. Moreover, controversies have persisted between the eastern industrial and the southern and western agricultural regions of the nation over tariffs, which protect U.S. manufacturing while deterring trade in agricultural products such as wheat and cotton.

Even before Henry Clay came forward with a compromise tariff that placated South Carolina and thereby avoided the resort to arms threatened by both President Andrew Jackson[2] and the

2. Jackson concurred with Daniel Webster, noting that nullification was "incompatible with the existence of the Union, contradicted expressly by the letter of the Constitution, unauthorized by its spirit, inconsistent with every principle on which it was founded, and destructive of the great objective for which it was formed." Quoted in John M. Blum and others, *The National Experience* (Harcourt, Brace and World, 1963), p. 225.

South Carolina legislature, lines were drawn over the equally intensive "Bank war." At issue was the Bank of the United States, chartered by Congress in 1816 for twenty years. President Jackson raised the issue in his message to Congress soon after assuming office in 1829, holding that the concentration of such enormous economic power in the hands of one corporation endangered the democracy. When the bill authorizing the renewal of the charter came before him in 1832, he vetoed it.

While the bitter controversies over the tariff, banking and currency, and the nature of the Union were creating pro- and anti-Jackson camps, the issue of egalitarianism rapidly became the basis of a broad political movement. The movement arose as a response to the kidnapping of William Morgan of Batavia, New York, in 1826 allegedly by Freemasons. Morgan, a defector from the Masonic order, had written a book supposedly revealing its secrets. As news of his disappearance spread, mass protest meetings were held throughout the rural areas of western New York. The Anti-Masons contended that Morgan's kidnapping and assumed murder were not only an affront to all law-abiding citizens, but a direct challenge to the integrity of the republican form of government. "An injury to one member of society ... was an injury to all—and duty as well as interest required men to act."[3]

The movement was not purely political, but very much akin to a religious crusade. The evil to be eradicated was "the Monster Institution" of freemasonry that operated clandestinely to subvert the forces of good—that is, the common man. This overflowing of religion into politics[4] enabled the Anti-Masons "to identify the Masons with the foes of evangelical Protestantism."[5] For those who see anti-masonry as principally a reaction to a conspiracy of an

3. Lee Benson, *The Concept of Jacksonian Democracy: New York as a Test Case* (Atheneum, 1966), p. 16.

4. It does not seem accidental that anti-masonry was most successful in the areas of western New York noted for religious revivals and in later years benevolent movements. See Whitney R. Cross, *The Burned-Over District: The Social and Intellectual History of Enthusiastic Religion in Western New York, 1800–1850* (Cornell University Press, 1950).

5. Seymour Martin Lipset and Earl Raab, *The Politics of Unreason: Right-Wing Extremism in America, 1790–1970* (Harper and Row, 1970), p. 43.

aristocratic class, the movement is exemplary of fanatical right-wing extremism in American politics.[6]

Anti-masonry appears, however, to have been far more an agrarian, lower-class egalitarian movement than one of right-wing extremism, and a logical outgrowth of the republican ethos fostered in the early decades of the American experience.[7] In an age when economic and social position were to be earned, not inherited as in the rigid class systems of Europe, when the political arena became accessible to all classes of people, and when suffrage expanded rapidly, political mobilization of the lower classes was inevitable. At issue was the right of all citizens to participate equally and freely in the political process. "In essence the Antimasonic argument can be stated in this syllogism: Equal opportunity was the hallmark of a republican country. Freemasonry destroyed equal opportunity by secretly using its great powers to favor the interests of its members. Freemasonry, therefore, could not be permitted to exist in the republican United States."[8]

Anti-masonry had little impact on the New York elections in 1826, but during the next year numerous town and village committees passed resolutions declaring "Freemasons unfit for any office of confidence."[9] In 1828, Anti-Masons elected six state senators and seventeen assemblymen,[10] while their candidate in the gubernatorial race received over 12 percent of the vote. Although the new party did not enter the presidential contest that year, its presence was felt. As a consequence of their heated attack on the Jackson party—Jackson was a high Mason, as were many of the followers of his close associate, Martin Van Buren of New York—masonry became an issue in the election. President John Quincy Adams, the National Republican candidate, publicly disavowed any association with or belief in secret societies. As a result, Thurlow Weed and most other Anti-Masonic leaders endorsed Adams.

6. Ibid.
7. Benson, *Jacksonian Democracy*, pp. 19–20.
8. Ibid., p. 19.
9. Ibid., p. 21.
10. Lipset and Raab, *Politics of Unreason*, p. 41.

Shortly thereafter the party spread throughout New England and the mid-Atlantic states, establishing its strongest hold on the religious-minded Vermonters. In 1829 it ran second to the National Republicans in the state and in 1830 it forced the gubernatorial election into the legislature. By 1831 it had become the largest party in Vermont. It also thrived in Massachusetts and Pennsylvania. Yet it never flourished in New Hampshire or Maine or in New Jersey. The Anti-Masons seem to have filled a political void in the states where either Jackson sentiment was weakest—Vermont and Massachusetts—or Adams sentiment was weakest—New York and Pennsylvania.[11] The party became the "opposition" party in a number of essentially one-party states. Nevertheless, it was concern about the issues of masonry and secret societies—not the conduciveness of the political setting—that gave rise to the party and that was ultimately responsible for its demise. This fact was clearly revealed when the Anti-Masons entered national politics.

THE ELECTION OF 1832

With the Democrats united behind the incumbent Jackson and the National Republicans nominating Henry Clay, the major lines of division in the campaign of 1832 were established. An issue that Clay had assumed would work to his advantage, Jackson's bank charter veto, had just the opposite effect. If anything, it enhanced Jackson's position. In addition, the parties clashed over nullification and Clay's American plan for internal improvements. Yet the major parties failed to address the equally pressing issue raised by the Anti-Masons.

*The Anti-Mason Party.* On the heels of their extraordinary growth between 1829 and 1831, the Anti-Masons were determined to make a bid for national prominence. With Jackson as the symbol of the influence of masonry, and an anti-Jackson coalition with the National Republicans seemingly plausible, the Anti-Masons met

11. Richard P. McCormick, *The Second American Party System* (University of North Carolina Press, 1966), p. 73.

in Baltimore, in September 1831, in the first national party convention ever. They hoped to nominate as their candidate a man with broad political support, such as John McLean of Ohio, who could carry both Anti-Masonic and the National Republican constituencies.[12] McLean had notified the party leaders that his acceptance of the nomination would be contingent on there being no other opposition candidate in the campaign, but shortly before the convention he concluded that under no circumstances should he jeopardize his national appeal by accepting the nomination of an intense minority. The convention settled on William Wirt of Maryland.[13]

The National Republicans, while desiring Jackson's defeat, were not willing to pay the price of endorsing the Anti-Mason candidate. Thus, although the two parties out of power were able to arrange some coalitions on the state level,[14] they failed to form a national coalition. The fervor aroused by the single issue of masonry effectively prevented the Anti-Masonic party from compromising on the issue. The National Republicans were afraid to embrace the Anti-Mason cause, which would probably have undermined their appeal on other issues and alienated the many Masons within the party. The impossibility of a coalition was made all the more certain by Clay's unequivocal repudiation of the principles of the Anti-Masons following their convention.[15] In short, the issue of masonry overrode the great incentives the two opposition parties had to coalesce in their common goal of defeating Jackson. Left to their own resources, the Anti-Masons polled 8 percent of the

12. E. Malcolm Carroll, *Origins of the Whig Party* (Duke University Press, 1925), pp. 48–52. McLean had been postmaster general under Presidents James Monroe and John Quincy Adams and since 1829 associate justice of the U.S. Supreme Court.

13. Wirt was also aware of the possibility of a coalition of the anti-Jackson forces and ready to use his influence in support of Clay if the election went into the House of Representatives. Ibid., p. 52.

14. In New York, Anti-Masonic and National Republican support was given to a single list of electors with the understanding that if the ticket won, the electoral votes would go to either Clay or Wirt as circumstances might require to defeat Jackson. In Pennsylvania the National Republicans withheld their ticket and supported the Anti-Masons. A similar arrangement was made in the gubernatorial contest in Ohio. Ibid., p. 52.

15. Ibid., p. 51, note 70.

popular vote, winning a plurality—41 percent of the vote—only in Vermont.[16]

The election revealed that the Anti-Masons were unable to expand from their rural base and limited numbers of strong state organizations. With the demise of masonry in the mid-1830s, the party collapsed. Soon therafter much of its membership merged into the new Whig party, which rapidly became the second major national party.

### SIMILARITIES OF THE 1832 AND 1968 ELECTIONS

The conditions surrounding the significant third-party vote of 1832 closely approximate those in 1968, with one qualification. A small number of issues dominated the political scene, generating a general sense of tension and a high level of ideological and moral ferment. During the crisis period an intense minority emerged around one issue that they believed to be of great importance. The major parties, however, did not champion a view opposing that of the minority, as they did in 1968, but tried to avoid the issue of masonry altogether. This left a vacuum in which the third party— championing the cause of anti-masonry, and demanding an end to secret societies and the actualization of the American egalitarian dream—grew rapidly. Only in their default, then, did the major parties take the same position on masonry. Yet their inaction is precisely what alienated the intense minority from both major parties.

## Settlement and the Restriction of Slavery

The Democratic-Whig alignment that emerged after the election of 1832 survived for two decades. It collapsed in the middle of the nineteenth century, when the settlement of the frontier territories and the inseparable questions of slavery and the role of the federal government became the focus of an intense national conflict. An

---

16. The Anti-Masonic ticket drew a larger share of the vote in Pennsylvania, where Wirt polled 42 percent of the votes in a two-way contest with Jackson.

unprecedented series of third parties surfaced in the presidential contests from 1848 through 1860, reflecting the inability of the major parties to deal with the conflict. In the span of four elections four significant third-party votes were registered and a new major party appeared. The Free Soil party of 1848, the American party in 1856, and the Constitutional Union party and the Breckinridge Democrats of 1860 amassed substantial third-party votes. The Republican party replaced the Whigs as the second major party in 1856. The issues in contention divided both major parties and were ultimately resolved through civil war. Although the war did not remove racial animosity, it did remove slavery as a controversial political issue and provided a "northern solution" to settlement of the territories.

### THE CONFLICT EVOLVES

While the westward expansion of a young and vigorous nation across a virgin continent[17] may be too encompassing as an explanation of the unique qualities of the American character and institutions, that expansion clearly left its imprint on the nation. Each time new territories were considered for statehood, the balance between the slave culture of the South and the free society of the North was a divisive issue.[18] Settlement and statehood became the focal points of contention between the two distinct parts of the federal union. If the federation between the two sections had been limited to the original states, or even to the boundaries of 1820, the two might have found a peaceful means of accommodation.[19] But no accommodation could be reached in a period when the North was outpacing the South economically, and the two were competing to "conquer the West." By 1850 the territories in conten-

17. Frederick Jackson Turner, "The significance of the frontier in American History," *Annual Report of the American Historical Association for the year 1893*, pp. 199–227.

18. In the 1840s southerners began to see the implication of existing settlement patterns, and they became the central underlying issue in national politics. Roy F. Nichols, *The Stakes of Power, 1845–1877* (Hill and Wang, 1961), pp. 4–5.

19. Barrington Moore, Jr., *Social Origins of Dictatorship and Democracy* (Beacon, 1966), chap. 3

tion were greater in size than all the existing states. Since it was widely believed that slavery and a free labor market could not be intermingled, slave interests would have to be allocated entire tracts of this land.[20] The South needed new states for economic expansion as well as to maintain a political balance with the North in the national government.

In 1819 the issue of slavery erupted when the territory of Missouri, settled primarily by Kentucky and Tennessee slavery sympathizers, petitioned for entry into the Union as a slave state. Until this time, slavery had not been a matter of national controversy, and the two sections had maintained a balance within the federal system. The divisive debate centered on an amendment to the Missouri enabling bill proposed by a representative from New York that would have prohibited additional slaves from entering Missouri and provided for the gradual emancipation of those already there. The northern majority in the House passed the bill, but it was defeated in the Senate. With neither side willing to concede, the issue was not reconciled until acceptance of the Missouri Compromise of 1820. Under the compromise Maine was admitted as a free state to balance the entry of Missouri as a slave state. The growing power of the North was reflected in the provision that slavery would not be extended north of the 36°30′ latitude in the remaining areas of the Louisiana Territories. Hence it would be restricted to the Arkansas Territory, approximately one-fifth of the area still held by the federal government. The compromise reconciled the two sections temporarily, but the South retained a potential veto through its power in the Senate.

The annexation of Texas and the Mexican War reopened the conflict from 1846 through 1849. Not only was the entry of a single slave state at issue, but also the formula by which all remaining territories were to be settled and admitted to the Union. In the short span of four years, during the Polk administration (1845–

20. For an argument that the clash was over the survival of two distinct cultures, see Eugene D. Genovese, *The Political Economy of Slavery* (Vintage, 1967); and Eric Foner, *Free Soil, Free Labor, Free Men: The Ideology of the Republican Party Before the Civil War* (Oxford University Press, 1970).

49), the United States had acquired an enormous body of land—in the northwest the Oregon Territory, to the south the Republic of Texas, to the west and southwest California and the New Mexico and Utah territories.

The Wilmot Proviso of 1846 placed the slavery issue in the center of the annexation debates. As controversy surrounding the acquisitions from Mexico developed in the House of Representatives, David Wilmot, a Pennsylvania Democrat, introduced an amendment to a bill appropriating funds to facilitate the acquisitions requiring that "neither slavery nor involuntary servitude shall ever exist in any part of said territory." The amendment passed the House twice but was defeated in the Senate. The two-year debate over the proviso placed the question of slavery expansion at the core of all the questions related to the settlement of the West, the role of the federal government in the development of the economy, and the relations between the North and the South.[21] By 1848 the slavery restrictionists had rallied behind the proviso, making it the focal point of their drive to limit slavery to its existing boundaries.

THE ELECTION OF 1848

Political reality inhibited both major parties in 1848 from making any blatant appeals to the slavery restriction faction. The Democratic party was heavily dependent on southern support for its national dominance. The Whig party, with its fragile coalition of Cotton Whigs and Conscience Whigs, could ill afford to respond aggressively to the growing restrictionist sentiment.[22] Although many of the northern Whigs and some Democrats were in sympathy with the restrictionists, their overriding concern for other political, economic, or social goals tied them to the existing party coalitions.

*The Free Soil Party.* In the months preceding the major party conventions, before the candidates and platforms that skirted the

21. Joseph G. Rayback, *Free Soil: The Election of 1848* (University Press of Kentucky, 1970), chap. 2.
22. Ibid., chap. 7; see also Edgar E. Robinson, *The Evolution of American Political Parties* (Harcourt, Brace, 1924), pp. 135–37.

slavery and settlement issue had been adopted, the restrictionists in both parties were open to compromise, hoping to remain within their respective folds.[23] Only when their positions had been rejected did they turn to the third party being organized by the Liberty men, who had first appeared in the 1844 presidential election, polling 2 percent of the popular vote. The Liberty men had already laid the groundwork for the Free Soil party, calling for a "Free Territory Convention."[24] When they eventually met in the Free Soil convention in Buffalo, the radicals on the slavery issue and the more pragmatic politicos reached an accord. The defecting Barnburners of the Democratic party gained the nomination for former President Van Buren; the Liberty men had carte blanche in writing the platform, a document that fully reflected restrictionist views.[25]

Thus the clash over the extension of slavery was brought before the public in the 1848 presidential campaign through a third party. Supporters of the Liberty party, the Conscience Whigs, and the Barnburners coalesced in the Free Soil party behind a slavery restriction platform with the Wilmot Proviso as its theme: "neither slavery nor involuntary servitude should ever exist in any territory that might be obtained from Mexico."

The party polled 10 percent nationally (it won only a few hundred votes in the South), and 14 percent of the popular votes in the free states. Its support reached 29 percent in Vermont, 28 percent in Massachusetts, and 26 percent in Van Buren's home state of New York.

---

23. "Barnburners in New York still appeared slightly hopeful that the [Democratic] delegates in Baltimore would prove amenable to reason. They were prepared, in return for recognition as the legitimate delegation from the Empire State, to allow the Democracy almost full latitude in nominating any candidate except Polk, provided always that no southern test was applied. For the sake of party unity they would not press their Provisoist demands. At the same time, they were mentally prepared to revolt if their minimal conditions were not satisfied. Conscience Whigs were likewise ready to remain with their party. Their support, however, was contingent upon the nomination of an antiextensionist—a harder condition than the Barnburners imposed, a condition which few expected to be met." Rayback, *Free Soil*, pp. 184–85.

24. Ibid., p. 183.

25. Foner, *Free Soil, Free Labor, Free Men*, p. 125.

Van Buren campaigned on the Free Soil platform, demanding the restriction of slavery, a homestead act for free settlers, and federally sponsored internal improvements. In contrast, the Whigs campaigned behind the Louisiana slaveholder—guilty by association in the eyes of the slavery restrictionists—and Mexican War hero, General Zachary Taylor. The Democrats offered a counterpart to Taylor in Lewis Cass of Michigan, who opposed the Wilmot Proviso and resolved not to be ensnarled in the controversy over slavery. The majority of the electorate appear to have either rejected or been unconcerned about the expansion of slavery. Neither the southerner Taylor nor the accommodating Cass would take a strong position in favor of either restricting slavery or unconditionally opening the territories to slavery. Of course, for the restrictionists, equivocation was no solution at all. As a result, the Free Soil party was able to capitalize on the views of a very intense minority on a highly visible issue.

*Aftermath.* Although the Free Soilers must have appeared to the majority of the electorate as uncompromising extremists, their strong vote indicated that the question of slavery in the territories could no longer be brushed aside. Otherwise, as many had always feared, it might polarize the populace along geographic lines and destroy the Union. The major parties attempted to remove the issue from partisan politics through adoption of the Compromise of 1850. In one dramatic move, led first by the eminent Whig Henry Clay and then by the Democrat Stephen A. Douglas, they sought to resolve the questions surrounding slavery in the new territories: California would be admitted as a free state; territorial governments, without any restriction on slavery, would be provided for the remaining Mexican cession; Texas would relinquish its claim to portions of eastern New Mexico; the federal government would assume the public debt incurred by Texas prior to annexation; the District of Columbia would no longer be used as a depot in the interstate slave trade; slavery would be abolished in the District of Columbia only with the consent of its residents and the state of Maryland and with compensation to the slaveholders; a more rigorous fugitive-slave act would be adopted; and Congress would affirm that it had no power to interfere with the interstate slave trade.[26]

An ardent minority of slaveholders, such as William L. Yancey of Alabama, saw the compromise as a crushing blow to southern culture. Convinced that the position of the South in the Union was lost, they called for immediate secession. In the North the extreme restrictionists and abolitionists rejected the plan as an implicit reaffirmation of the legitimacy of the institution of slavery. Most voters, however, seem to have been satisfied. Admission of California as a free state ended debate over its status. The question of slavery in territories was defused with the relegation of future decisions to "local self-determination."

With wide acceptance of the compromise, the Free Soil vote in 1852 declined to just under 5 percent of the total popular vote. Politicians could read this outcome as a vote of no confidence for the Free Soilers and henceforth ignore the party. In the election campaign the Democrats had openly embraced the compromise and the Whigs had accepted it begrudgingly, but both had accepted it. It must have seemed that the sectional conflict could be resolved through the normal avenues of bargaining between sectional leaders and that once again the country could turn its attention to other matters.

THE ELECTION OF 1856

Local self-determination did not defuse the slavery issue, however, and in the four years following the election of 1852, the country underwent a major realignment of political forces. The Whigs, unable to provide a viable program for dealing with the question of slavery restriction, collapsed as a national organization. At the same time the Democrats, trying to appease their southern constituency, lost appreciable northern support. Meanwhile, the Free Soilers, under the Republican banner,[27] grew in strength to

26. Blum and others, *National Experience*, p. 278.
27. See Ronald P. Formisano, *The Birth of Mass Political Parties: Michigan, 1827–1861* (Princeton University Press, 1971), chaps. 12–14.

become the second major party nationally and the majority party in the North. The erstwhile southern Whigs were estranged from both groups: they were strongly opposed to the newly constituted Republican party of the North, yet they found little consolation in the position taken by their ancient rivals the Democrats. Hence by 1856 they had turned to the ostensibly nativist, but by this time defensively southern, new American party.

The sectional cleavage was reopened in January 1854 when the Kansas-Nebraska Act was introduced in Congress by Stephen A. Douglas, Democratic senator from Illinois. The bill was designed to open the plat country west of Missouri and Iowa, the remaining areas of the Louisiana Purchase.[28] "Popular sovereignty"—the 1850 rule applicable in the New Mexico and Utah territories—was to be the means of determining whether slavery would be tolerated. Under pressure from southern congressmen, Douglas incorporated amendments to his bill splitting the territory into Kansas and Nebraska and repealing the Missouri Compromise prohibition of slavery above the 36°30′ latitude. With the aid of the Pierce administration the bill was passed.

Outcries against the Kansas-Nebraska Act, Douglas, and the "slave powers" spread rapidly across the North. Slavery restrictionists were outraged by the abrogation of the Missouri Compromise, the law that had guaranteed free lands in the vast Nebraska territories for over three decades.[29] In the midterm elections of 1854 the combined anti-Nebraska forces, some of whom assumed the party name "Republican," elected 108 of the 234 House members in the Thirty-fourth Congress. Sectional animosities were further aggravated in the territorial elections, when Missourians crossed into Kansas to vote illegally, providing the winning margin for proslavery candidates. Border clashes followed between the abolitionist and slavery factions and quickly escalated into open warfare. In May 1856 a party of Missourians invaded and sacked

28. This region had to be settled before northern railroad interests, including many of Douglas's Chicago backers, could hope to win a northern route to the West through Chicago, as opposed to the more feasible southern route under consideration.

29. Nichols, *Stakes of Power*, p. 54.

the free-soil town of Lawrence, Kansas. John Brown, a fanatical abolitionist, retaliated against slavery sympathizers by murdering and mutilating five settlers. Federal troops intervened, but too late. Blood had been spilled on both sides. Hostility overflowed onto the floor of Congress when Congressman Preston S. Brooks of South Carolina caned Senator Charles Sumner of Massachusetts to unconsciousness. The attack was provoked by Sumner's inflammatory antislavery speech "The Crime against Kansas," given two days earlier, in which he bitterly denounced Brooks's uncle, Senator Andrew Pickens Butler of South Carolina.

*The Republican Party.* Because of these violent clashes and the growing sectional antagonism, no issue so dominated the public's attention during the 1856 campaign as slavery and settlement. The newly formed Republican party was able to coalesce anti-Nebraska men, free soilers, and abolitionists, as well as many Democrats and Whigs. With the frontier explorer John C. Frémont as its candidate, the party united behind a platform closely approximating the Free Soil platform of 1848. It focused on "bleeding Kansas," calling for containment of slavery, a homestead act for "free" settlers, and extensive internal improvement programs. The party won more than 33 percent of the popular vote. Frémont carried all the free states except California, Illinois, Indiana, New Jersey, and Pennsylvania.

*The Democratic Party.* The Democratic party was able to sustain its sectional coalition and in turn control the presidency. It did so by nominating James Buchanan of Pennsylvania, who avoided entanglement in the Kansas-Nebraska debate by being out of the country, and whose views on slavery were not known. The platform called for "popular sovereignty" in the territories in hopes of skirting any internal party dispute over slavery. The strategy proved effective and Buchanan carried the electoral college with 174 votes, although the party's popular support dropped to under 46 percent of the total vote, reflecting a loss of support in the North to the Republicans from the previous election.

*The American Party.* The sectional cleavage was not the only issue prominent in the mid-1850s. A nativist Protestant antipathy to foreigners and Catholics led to the formation of the significant third party of 1856, the American party. In the months preceding the election, however, even the nationally visible and divisive issue of nativism was overshadowed by the deeper sectional split.

A number of nativist sects had arisen in the 1840s in response to the extensive tide of immigration, particularly of Catholics. These groups united in the early 1850s in a secret organization, the Order of the Star Spangled Banner. Refusing to provide information about their society, they were dubbed the "Know-Nothings." The movement, which spread throughout the states in the early 1850s, was particularly strong in the large urban areas of the North and the South. Immigrants were despised not only for their religious beliefs, but because they provided cheap competition in the labor market.[30] In the South, nativism was also a means of implicitly attacking northern economic and social institutions. Southerners began to see the unrestricted importation of cheap labor into the North as a key factor in the growing imbalance between the sections. In ten years the free states had gained fifty new representatives in the Congress.[31] For southerners, restricting the flow of immigrants (who were understandably unsympathetic to slavery) and disfranchising the foreign born were fundamental steps needed to redress the imbalance.

In 1854 the Know-Nothings won numerous local and state elections, claiming the allegiance of seventy-five congressmen, primarily from the South.[32] The most spectacular victory came in Massachusetts where they carried all state offices and a majority of the seats in the legislature. Convinced of their ability to carry the nation in 1856, the members of the state parties met in a national convention in 1855.

The southern contingent of the party was especially eager to capitalize on the nativist sentiment. In a period when northerners were flocking to the antislavery Republican party and the Demo-

30. Lipset and Raab, *Politics of Unreason*, pp. 47–59.
31. Wilfred E. Binkley, *American Political Parties: Their Natural History* (4th ed., Knopf, 1966), p. 194.
32. Blum and others, *National Experience*, p. 295.

crats were under attack for the Kansas-Nebraska Act, the Know-Nothing party gave southerners an issue with which they could both counteract the abolitionists and unify forces across the nation. The strength of the nativist crusade was greatly diminished, however, when the Kansas-Nebraska issue brought slavery to the fore in party affairs. When the southern organizers of the party's nominating convention forced through a proslavery resolution, Henry Wilson, the newly elected senator from Massachusetts, led a northern walkout.

The convention proceeded, naming itself the American party and nominating Millard Fillmore, the one-time Whig President, as its candidate. The party's appeal, however, was restricted to southern Whigs who sought an alternative to joining the escalating controversy over slavery. Nationally, the third-party vote totaled 21 percent, but the vote was essentially from traditional Whig constituencies in southern and border states. Of the votes cast in the free states, only 9 percent were for Fillmore, of those cast in the eleven southern states 42 percent, and of those cast in the border states of Maryland, Delaware, Kentucky, and Missouri 49 percent. In Massachusetts, where the Know-Nothings had won overwhelmingly in 1854, the vote for Fillmore was only 12 percent, whereas the Republicans received 65 percent. The election focused on the sectional cleavage caused by the issue of slavery extension, with nativism attracting mostly former Whigs, who fit neither into the new Republican fold nor with their traditional Democratic rivals.

The victory of Buchanan, the compromise candidate on slavery, could not hide the serious national split over the issue reflected in the rise of the distinctly sectional Republican party. After the election the Republicans remained adamant in their drive to bring "freedom" and free men to the West, without proposing to mollify the South.

## THE ELECTION OF 1860

The sectional dispute was further aggravated after 1856 by the Supreme Court's highly publicized Dred Scott decision, which hinged on whether or not protection of federal citizenship were

applicable to Negroes crossing into free states. Chief Justice Roger
B. Taney in the majority opinion declared Negroes inferior beings
with "no rights which any white man was bound to respect."[33] He
also declared the Missouri Compromise unconstitutional, arguing
that Congress had no power to regulate slavery in the territories.
With the decision the situation became frozen and slavery became
constitutionally enshrined. Southerners rejoiced in this vindication
by the Court, while more and more northerners were provoked
into joining the drive to rid the country of the "slave power."

A second factor in the continuing state of apprehension was an
intensifying dispute over Kansas, whose bid for entry into the
Union under the Lecompton constitution President Buchanan endorsed. Opponents of the constitution saw it as the product of a
proslavery conspiracy brought about through a fraudulent election. They contended that the constitution violated the spirit if not
the letter of the doctrine of popular sovereignty and they objected
strongly to the provision that no future amendments could inhibit
slavery in the state. Even when Buchanan made the congressional
vote on the Lecompton constitution a test of party loyalty, the
Democrats split along sectional lines. Stephen Douglas, the author
of the original Kansas-Nebraska Act, led the opposition. In spite of
the efforts by Douglas, the bill cleared the Senate under heavy administration pressure, but failed in the northern-dominated House.
Of more importance than the fate of the constitution was the debate over it that openly split the Democrats along sectional lines.

The Lincoln-Douglas debates in the 1858 Senate race in Illinois
accentuated the split. Douglas, adhering to the Democratic program, would not condemn slavery. Instead he argued that slavery
could be excluded from the territories by not adopting the strict
slave codes being demanded by many slaveholders. Without such
codes he, and to his ultimate ruin many southerners, believed that
slavery could not thrive in the territories. Hence, Douglas con-
ceded that under his program slavery had little likelihood of success in the territories, irrespective of its sanction under existing
federal law.

33. Ibid., p. 312.

These events set the stage for another sectional clash in 1860. The controversy was brought to an emotional climax by the attempted invasion of the South by an armed force led by John Brown, who hoped to trigger an insurrection among the slaves.[34] Impractical though his plan may have been, his abortive raid on the federal arsenal at Harper's Ferry, Virginia, in October 1859, had serious repercussions. In the South the raid heightened the growing fears of a slave revolt, especially since Brown had received financial and spiritual aid from New York and New England philanthropists. In the North Brown became a martyr among abolitionists. For the nation as a whole the raid served to drive deeper the wedge between the sections.

*The Breckinridge Democrats.* By 1860 the slavery issue was irreconcilable, and following the pattern of the Whigs, the Democrats split along regional lines. When the southern faction felt their cause was forsaken, they walked out of the Democratic convention. The remaining northerners nominated Senator Douglas of Illinois, who attempted to accommodate both sections by advocating that the Supreme Court be the final arbiter on the question of slavery in the territories. Douglas promptly took to the stump to warn the nation of the impending danger. Only his program of popular sovereignty was viable, he argued; disunion and secession could only result in ruin. His warning fell on deaf ears. After tirelessly spreading his message through the South, West, and East, he received a disappointing 30 percent of the popular vote, dispersed across the states in such a manner that it gained only 4 percent of the electoral college votes.

The southern Democrats regrouped into a new political party and nominated John C. Breckinridge of Kentucky. Breckinridge countered Douglas by asserting that the federal government must protect "the rights of property" in the territories through a strict body of slave codes. Anything short of explicit federal protection would spell doom for slavery. On this platform the southern Democrats carried nine states of the South, receiving 18 percent of the popular vote and 24 percent of the electoral college votes.

34. Nichols, *Stakes of Power*, p. 74.

The Republicans did not change appreciably from their northern-western axis of support of 1856. Their platform affirmed their hostility toward slavery, promising to confine it to the South. In addition they promised economic aid for industrial development in the East and for westward expansion for free settlers. Although its popular vote rose only to 40 percent—6 percent over that of 1856—the party carried all the northern and western states and received 59 percent of the electoral college votes. In the short period encompassing two elections, the Republicans rose from obscurity to the presidency.

*The Constitutional Union Party.* Set between the clearly sectional major parties, both geographically and substantively, was the Constitutional Union party. The party had a singular theme, that of preserving "the Constitution of the Country, the Union of the States, and the Enforcement of the Laws."[35] On the basis of a plea for national unity, John Bell of Tennessee campaigned as the party's presidential nominee. He appealed mainly to those caught in the sectional split, particularly those in the upper South. Nationally, he received 13 percent of the popular vote. He carried Kentucky, Tennessee, and Virginia, with his greatest support coming from old Whig and American party quarters.[36]

With Lincoln's victory came the secession of the states of the Deep South and open conflict, the formation of the Confederacy, and the Civil War. Only in this fashion was the issue of the expansion of slavery resolved.

SIMILARITIES OF THE 1848, 1856, 1860,
AND 1968 ELECTIONS

The prime criterion for significant third-party voting, the presence of severe political crisis, existed almost continuously from the mid-1840s to the mid-1860s. Only in the early 1850s was the issue of the expansion of slavery temporarily defused through adoption

35. Kirk H. Porter and Donald B. Johnson, *National Party Platforms 1840–1968* (University of Illinois Press, 1970), p. 30.
36. Walter Dean Burnham, *Presidential Ballots, 1836–1892* (Johns Hopkins Press, 1955).

of the Compromise of 1850. Correspondingly, only in 1852 did the usual two-party pattern of presidential competition prevail. In the other three antebellum elections, large and aroused minorities were sufficiently estranged from the major parties to provide the basis for significant third-party efforts. Only in 1848, however, was the alignment of forces approximately like that in 1968. In this election an intense minority—the Free Soilers—took an extreme position while the major parties equivocated, directing their campaigns as much as possible toward other issues.

In 1856 and 1860, virtually the entire electorate was divided by the repeatedly exacerbated controversy over the expansion of slavery, aligning itself into distinct, hostile camps. In 1856 the Democrats managed to retain their national coalition, but they were severely challenged on the one side by the restrictionist Republicans and on the other by the equally staunch nativist Americans. By 1860, little room remained for compromise. Principle and moral absolutes were the only subjects of political dialogue.

As the level of conflict reached its highest peak ever, the electorate was severely polarized, and the normal incentives to coalesce inherent in the electoral system were effectively checked. With the electorate split four ways, no bargains could be struck across sectional lines that would attract a majority of the voters. In short, with the breakdown in the second half of the 1850s of the normal give-and-take and tempered style characteristic of American politics, the two-party system collapsed. The era is extraordinary not because the preconditions to third-party voting were unmet, but because they were met many times over. By the end of the decade, national coalitions were untenable and not one, but two, three, and even four intense minorities had entered the field.

## Reconstruction

The Civil War ended the practice of slavery, but not racially based conflicts. In the postwar period, radical Republicans and white southerners struggled to determine who would rule the defeated states of the Confederacy and what the role of the South would be in the reunited nation. The nation's economy was in disarray, brought on by the return to peacetime pursuits, overextension of the railroads into the West, the Panic of 1873, and a concurrent financial crisis in Europe. These factors contributed to the reshuffling of forces within the major parties, and in large part to the gains made by the Democrats in the mid-term congressional elections of 1874. But the major issue—radical Republican domination over the South—"ten years after Appomattox . . . brought the country to the verge of civil war." The compromise between the leaders of the two regions that settled the political problems "tacitly allowed the restoration of white supremacy throughout the South and thus adjourned the whole problem of effective citizenship of Negroes."[37] It also caused untold damage to the integrity of the electoral system.

The election of 1876 produced no overwhelming majority for either side. With the country evenly divided, either position was a feasible election strategy, and the major parties took opposing stands. The choice was clearly between the Republicans symbolizing military control over the South, black enfranchisement, and rule by carpetbaggers and scalawags, and the Democrats pressing for a return to local self-rule—returning the South to the indigenous white leaders. The only group unrepresented were former slaves, and they were in no position to organize politically. The Democrats, advocating southern autonomy, apparently polled 51 percent of the popular vote to the Republicans' 48 percent in a disputed election marked by fraud on both sides.

CRISIS WITHOUT A THIRD PARTY

The depression of 1873 worked against the Republicans, and northern audiences grew less and less receptive to radical rule over the South in the postwar years. The important factor in the election of 1876 was the umbrella provided by the Democrats for dissidents on economic issues and on the question of continued military domination and Republican rule in the South; the resulting

37. Dahl, *Political Oppositions*, p. 52. See also J. G. Randall and David Donald, *The Civil War and Reconstruction* (2nd ed., D. C. Heath, 1961), p. 700.

coalition was able to challenge the Republicans seriously for the first time in over a decade. In short, the two major parties during the Reconstruction crisis so encompassed the issues in debate that they prevented the estrangement of any factions that might seek redress through a third-party movement.

## Agrarian Protest

"During the last third of the century, discontented farmers and urban workers formed a pool of recurring opposition to the policies of a national government that responded less and less to their demands and more and more to those of the new men of business, industry, and finance."[38] The conflict between the agrarian and corporate interests reached crisis proportions in the 1890s, affecting primarily the South and West in the early stages and culminating in a nationwide realignment of forces in 1896.

The principal points of contention were the lack of inexpensive investment capital for farmers and of cheap transportation for the shipment of farm produce to eastern markets. Both problems were accentuated by the depression following the bank panic of 1893. Farmers, increasingly frustrated by the currency and transportation systems, were unable to win governmental redress. As early as the 1870s farmers claimed, often with substantial evidence, that the railroads were making exorbitant and sometimes illegal profits through the grading, storing, and shipping of wheat, corn, and other produce. Ultimately, in their outrage against what they viewed as exploitation by the eastern "capitalists," the discontented farmers united.

Seeking relief from their financial woes, they first turned to the nonpolitical Grange, which had grown to nearly 900,000 members by 1875, concentrated in the north central states of Illinois, Wisconsin, Iowa, and Minnesota.[39] Soon, however, they turned to politics, and when the major parties refused to act aggressively on their behalf, they sought independent action. In the 1870s, agrarian

38. Dahl, *Political Oppositions*, p. 52.
39. Randall and Donald, *Civil War and Reconstruction*, p. 663.

candidates appeared in many midwestern and western states under a variety of party banners: Anti-Monopoly, Reform, Independent Reform, National Reform, Independent, People's Independent.[40] On the national level the farm groups combined with radical labor groups in 1880 to back the Greenback-Labor party, but the party's 308,578 votes represented only 3.5 percent of the total vote. Subsequently, many farmers returned to the major parties.

Both nonpartisan and bipartisan activity in the 1880s failed to resolve the farmers' plight. In 1888, members of the ostensibly nonpolitical but social, fraternal, and economic Farmers' Alliance organizations ran independent candidates in Texas, Arkansas, and South Carolina. The People's (Populist) party of Kansas elected a United States senator in that year, and Alliance candidates ran in South Dakota, Minnesota, North Dakota, Michigan, Iowa, Illinois, Indiana, and Colorado. By 1890, independent farmer parties were competing throughout the South and West.

Most Americans, however, still appeared to be concerned with other matters. Industrial centers of the Northeast were expanding, the urban proletariat was beginning to organize, immigrant labor continued to pour into the country, and large corporations grew in number and strength unchecked by any countervailing forces. Both major parties, whose constituencies coalesced primarily around religious, ethnic, social, and regional issues,[41] revered the free enterprise industrial system and with it the notion of minimum governmental interference in economic activities. Only on the issue of tariffs did their views on the role of government diverge.

The Republicans, as the avowed representatives of eastern wealth, appealed to both capitalists and workers, proclaiming high tariffs as a means of expanding the economy and thus of creating new jobs. Conversely, the Democrats sought drastic reductions of the tariffs to promote agricultural exports.

In practice, few Democrats were enthusiastic about reductions large enough actually to benefit farmers. When Democratic Presi-

40. Carl C. Taylor, *The Farmers' Movement 1620–1920* (American Book, 1953), p. 176.

41. Paul Kleppner, *The Cross of Culture: A Social Analysis of Midwestern Politics, 1850–1900* (Free Press, 1970).

dent Grover Cleveland proposed a broad tariff reduction in 1887
—aimed more at reducing the large surplus in the national treasury
than at aiding the farmer—he faced strong opposition from his
party's congressional leaders. The Congress essentially nullified the
reduction aspects of the tariff bill.

## THE ELECTION OF 1892

That no substantial effort was made to alleviate the plight of
farmers indicates that the leaders of the major parties, particularly
those outside the West and South, were not willing to change the
economic order in order to meet agrarian demands. Congress failed
to pass a "subtreasury plan" devised by the leaders of the Southern
Alliance to provide monetary relief for farmers through a system
of local banks and warehouses operated by the federal government.
Not even the support of many Alliance organizations in the election of sympathetic congressmen in 1890 brought positive action
on the plan. As conditions deteriorated, with foreclosures increasing, prices falling, and political leaders refusing aid, the bewildered
farmers grew more receptive to an appeal from a new party.

Enthusiasm for a new party was not universal. In the one-party
South, racial antagonism could still be called on effectively by the
Democrats to override the most pressing economic needs of the
poor whites. Not surprisingly, Leonidas L. Polk of North Carolina,
the influential president of the Southern Alliance, refused to com-
mit himself to the third-party movement that was beginning to
swell in the West, in hopes that the Democrats would adopt a
populist platform in 1892.[42] Only when the Democrats failed to
placate the farmers in either their platform or their choice of nominee did Polk openly join the Populist party. James B. Weaver,
who eventually became the party's candidate, opposed a third-
party campaign until the major parties had made their nominations.

Ignoring the warnings of their western and southern members,
both the Democrats and Republicans nominated representatives of
the eastern industrial establishment in 1892. The Republicans ran

42. John D. Hicks, *The Populist Revolt: A History of the Farmers' Alliance and
the People's Party* (University of Nebraska Press, 1961), p. 240.

the incumbent Benjamin Harrison, and the Democrats former President Cleveland. The message was clear enough to farmers across the South and West: their interests would again go untended. In the campaign Cleveland and Harrison chose to debate the old issue of tariffs. The major parties took the same position—preservation of the status quo—on the fundamental issue of the role of private corporations versus government control of the economy.

*The Populist Party.* With the exclusion of agrarians from the major party tickets, attention quickly focused on the Populists' convention, held in Omaha in July. The party's platform included the main agrarian demands that had been voiced during the preceding decades: governmental ownership of the major means of transportation, particularly the railroads, reform in the banking system including expansion of currency, and reform in land policies. The convention moved on to nominate Weaver for the presidency and Ben Terrell of Texas as his running mate.

The election was a disappointment for Populists who anticipated strong support from farmers, organized labor, and reformers of all kinds. The party received 8.5 percent of the popular vote, most of it from the politically aware members of farm organizations. It did best in the West, gaining 67 percent of the vote in Nevada, 57 percent in Colorado, 48 percent in Kansas, and 38 percent in South Dakota; in Alabama and Texas the party vote reached 36 percent and 24 percent, respectively. The Weaver vote, the largest third-party vote since before the Civil War, indicated the depth of the cleavage between the farmers of the West and South and the rapidly growing industrial mainstream of American society.

*Aftermath.* The resolution of the agrarian-industrial conflict was very different from the solution of the conflict over slavery. After the Panic of 1893 the challenge to the ruling corporate capitalists grew in intensity. By 1896 the clash of farmers and, to a limited extent, urban workers with the eastern industrial interests had been felt throughout the nation and had brought about a realignment of voters within the major parties.[43] The controversy

43. E. E. Schattschneider, *The Semi-Sovereign People* (Holt, Rinehart and Winston, 1960), chap. 5.

over the role of the federal government in the regulation of the economy and the concomitant issue of industrial versus agrarian interests remained the overriding issues, but they were now dealt with within the two-party framework. On one side stood the Republicans, reflecting the eastern capitalists; on the other stood the Democrat William Jennings Bryan, primarily advocating programs to aid farmers and thus winning the endorsement of the Populists.

The corporate interests prevailed, firmly entrenching the Republicans as the dominant party in national politics until the New Deal era.[44]

### SIMILARITIES OF THE 1892 AND 1968 ELECTIONS

The importance of a few issues, divisions of public opinion, and positions represented by the major parties leading to the appearance of the Populist party of 1892 match the basic pattern of third-party voting. Who was to control the national economy—the government or the capitalists—and what the role of farmers was to be became divisive issues between 1891 and 1896, especially in the South and West. In 1892 the electorate divided into a vast majority within the major parties and an intense minority that went unrepresented. When both major parties chose the prevailing majority view, defending the status quo, the farmers resorted to a third-party strategy to gain a hearing for their position. By 1896 the public was no longer divided into a vast majority and an intense minority, but into a Republican majority and a very large Democratic minority. With Bryan's candidacy the major parties offered contrasting solutions to the major issues. In fact, few major-party candidates have aroused the electorate to such extremes of admiration and scorn as did Bryan, and seldom have the major parties seemed so far apart on leading issues. Consequently, as in the period after Appomattox, the two major parties in 1896 offered sufficiently contrasting positions to preclude any significant third-party vote.

44. See Walter Dean Burnham, "The Changing Shape of the American Political Universe," *American Political Science Review*, vol. 59 (March 1965), pp. 7–28; and, Robert H. Wiebe, *The Search for Order, 1877–1920* (Hill and Wang, 1967).

## Corporate Regulation and
## Government Responsiveness

Demand for political and economic reform grew during the first decade of the twentieth century, becoming the focal point of controversy in the second decade. By the latter half of the administration of William Howard Taft, the public was aroused by the domination of the economy by giant trusts, the deplorable conditions of industrial labor, and rampant political corruption. With the issues kept in the limelight by such writers as Upton Sinclair, David Graham Phillips, Lincoln Steffens, and Samuel Hopkins Adams, the public was stirred to action.

Although the movement drew support from the old Populist constituency and advocated many of its programs for direct democracy, it was not based on agrarian interests. Rather, the reformists sprang from the new middle class of urban society, and their numbers included many of the established leaders who had been replaced by the new industrial elite.[45]

Reformers were concerned with the abuses of power by business and political leaders, and they feared the deep schisms these were causing throughout the land. The homogeneity characteristic of the tranquil agrarian past was rapidly changing to class polarization. Hence, "they feared the society would fragment, that basic conflict between the new poor and the new rich would split it apart."[46] The reformers believed that orderly change was possible through rational planning and democratic processes, that the failures and shortcomings of business were not inherent in the system but due to lack of foresight and rational planning.[47] For them, "reform became a technical question. Good and evil corresponded to

45. Richard Hofstadter, *The Age of Reform: From Bryan to F.D.R.* (Vintage, 1955), p. 144.
46. Michael Rogin, *The Intellectuals and McCarthy: The Radical Specter* (M.I.T. Press, 1967), p. 193.
47. See Samuel P. Hays, *Conservation and the Gospel of Efficiency: The Progressive Conservation Movement, 1890–1920* (Harvard University Press, 1956).

knowledge and ignorance, not to the struggle of one class or group against another."[48]

Their view came to prominence at a time when class conflict was playing an important role in Europe as well as in the United States. The most noted, and by many the most feared, of the native groups engaged in the class struggle was the Industrial Workers of the World, a revolutionary syndicalist labor union movement that originated in Chicago in 1905. The IWW or, as its members were commonly known, the Wobblies planned a world revolution based on the union of all wage earners. Their straightforward strategy called for "a series of strikes, leading to a general strike which would force the capitalists to capitulate. Thus the IWW was to be both the embryo of the new society and the revolutionary instrument for achieving it."[49] For almost two decades the Wobblies preached and practiced class conflict, organizing workers from the lumber camps of the Northwest to the migrant labor routes across the Midwest, and becoming infamous for their frequent resort to confrontation and violence.

In the xenophobic reaction that swept the nation during and after World War I, the Wobblies were one of the main targets of government suppression. In 1918 the federal government charged 101 Wobblies with sabotage and conspiracy in relation to the war effort. Their trial lasted a record five months, but the jury in less than one hour found all of the defendants guilty. "Although 101 defendants were at the bar, it was an organization, indeed, a philosophy, that was being prosecuted."[50]

The Wobblies usually stayed clear of elective politics. The self-proclaimed political arm of the union movement in the United States was the American Socialist party. The leading figure of the party, Eugene V. Debs, rejected the accommodations with capitalism being made by Samuel Gompers and his American Federa-

48. Rogin, *Intellectuals and McCarthy*, p. 199.
49. Paul F. Brissenden, *The Story of Syndicalism in the United States* (1920), pp. 351–52, cited in Patrick Renshaw, *The Wobblies: The Story of Syndicalism in the United States* (Anchor, 1968), p. 1.
50. Renshaw, *The Wobblies*, p. 177.

tion of Labor (AFL). Rather, he "favored the formation of a new federation of revolutionary industrial unions."[51] While never succeeding in this aim, the Socialists were instrumental in bringing many issues important to the working class before the electorate.

### THE ELECTION OF 1912

The growing polarization along class lines won for the reformist cause the support of much of the electorate. Offering an alternative to class conflict, reformers proposed that government act as an unprejudiced arbiter between competing interests. The state would be neutral; it would be administered by experts and would regulate the economy for the mutual benefit of all. The reformers' second theme, which struck at corruption and machine-controlled politics, called for more direct public participation in the governmental process through adoption of the recall, the referendum, direct party primaries, and direct election of U.S. senators.

In the years immediately preceding the election of 1912, the issues of government responsiveness and the regulation of trusts had become the leading and interrelated concerns of the electorate. Hence, both major parties could be expected to turn to reformist candidates. The Democrats, being out of power, made their choice with relative ease; they nominated Woodrow Wilson. Although Wilson was not from within the Democratic establishment, and not the choice of western agrarians, his image as reform governor of New Jersey made him an ideal head of the party ticket.

The Republicans were in a far more difficult position. Between 1901 and 1909 the party had come to symbolize reform under the "trust-busting," conservation, and direct-democracy programs supported by Theodore Roosevelt. He was succeeded in 1909 by his secretary of war, William Howard Taft, a man also sympathetic to reform. But Taft's actions in office quickly canceled his reformist credentials. Public interest in regulation of corporations, direct democracy, and aid to industrial workers was increasing, yet Taft became identified with the business elite by supporting high tariffs.

51. James Weinstein, *The Decline of Socialism in America, 1912–1925* (Vintage, 1969), p. 32.

In his reluctance to join George Norris and the insurgents in Congress in their battle to strip Speaker of the House Joseph G. Cannon of his dictatorial powers, Taft became identified with political bossism. Finally in his implied attack on Roosevelt's conservation and trust-busting programs, he was seen as the representative of the Old Guard Republicans.

A sure indication that Taft was out of step with the electorate was the defeat suffered by many of the Old Guard in the midterm election of 1910. For the first time since 1892, Democrats elected a majority in the House of Representatives, and they captured numerous local and state offices, including the governorships of New Jersey and New York.

The breach between the reformers and Old Guard grew with Taft's purge of Roosevelt appointees, his split with Roosevelt on both domestic and foreign policies, the growing public animosity toward the Taft administration, and Roosevelt's political ambitions. By 1912 the one-time comrades had severed all ties, and Roosevelt challenged Taft for the Republican party nomination.

There is nothing unusual about a hotly contested nominating battle within a major party, and seldom does the losing faction attempt to break away and initiate a new party. Yet the blatant power play by Taft in gaining control of the Republican convention in 1912 so offended the reform wing of the party that Roosevelt was able to lead a walkout. In the preferential primaries held in thirteen states in 1912, 36 delegate seats had gone to La Follette, 48 to Taft, and 278 to Roosevelt. The reformers saw this as an overwhelming endorsement of their programs and candidate and counted on a sizable portion of the delegate seats at the Republican convention. The Republican national committee, controlled by the incumbent Taft forces, allotted 235 of the 256 contested seats to Taft delegates. The challenged delegates were allowed to vote on their own credentials, and to no one's surprise the Taft supporters won. The convention proceeded in short order to renominate Taft on the first ballot.[52]

*The TR Progressives.* The Roosevelt men bolting the Repub-

52. Blum, *National Experience*, pp. 545–46.

lican convention regrouped in the Progressive party, meeting in convention in August 1912. Roosevelt was nominated as the party's presidential candidate, a reform platform was adopted, and "Onward, Christian Soldiers" became its marching song. Roosevelt's program of new nationalism called for the regulation of corporations, honesty and integrity in government, and direct democracy through presidential primaries, the initiative and referendum, and the popular election of U.S. senators.

Despite his formal split with the Republican party, Roosevelt was able to draw on Republican machinery at the state level, particularly in the North and West, and wherever reformers had power at the local level. Thus, the Progressives were in many ways only a splinter group of an existing major party.

Under the Progressive banner, Roosevelt polled 27 percent of the popular vote, running second to Wilson. Taft was left with only 23 percent of the popular vote, a smaller proportion than had ever been received by a Republican party presidential nominee.

*The Socialist Party of America.* As the reformers were being absorbed into the mainstream of American politics, more and more people on the fringe came to subscribe to the theory of class conflict, and to the Socialist party. These were not the urban industrial proletariat that Marxists might expect, but the agrarians, miners, and lumberjacks. As the political crisis over corporate domination, industrial capitalism, and corrupt politics grew graver, the Socialists were able to expand their ranks to their highest point ever. Believing that "society is divided into warring groups and classes, based upon material interests," and that "American political parties are the expression of economic class interests,"[53] the Socialists found it easy to differentiate themselves from the reformers. For them, reforms sought by the Progressives were little more than cosmetics to make an inherently decadent system more attractive. While the reforms might possibly remove a few of the vile injustices resulting from capitalism, they did not strike at the heart of the problem: domination by the capitalist class.

With a position directly opposed to that of the major parties in

53. Porter and Johnson, *National Party Platforms*, p. 189.

1912, Eugene V. Debs, the Socialist candidate, polled some 900,000 or 6 percent of the popular vote. His support revealed the presence of a minority of Americans who were clearly outside the mainstream. Reminiscent of their Populist support in the 1890s, the agrarian radicals of Oklahoma gave Debs 17 percent of the state's vote, his highest state total. His vote reached 10 percent or more in the farming, mining, and lumbering states of Nevada, Montana, Arizona, Washington, California, and Idaho. In some urban areas such as Milwaukee, where the Socialist organization of Victor Berger was entrenched, Debs did well, but these were exceptions.

*Aftermath.* The third parties that prospered in 1912 lost their appeal in the wake of reform programs adopted by the Wilson administration. The Progressive party collapsed both for the lack of new issues and because its leader returned to the Republican fold and endorsed Charles Evans Hughes in the 1916 election.

The continuing growth of the Socialist party throughout 1904, 1908, and 1912 had made it appear that a distinctively leftist party was emerging in the United States. In 1916, however, the proportion of popular votes for the party declined by one-half. The replacement of Debs, the long-standing national party leader, by A. A. Benson surely contributed to this decline. But far more important was the aggressive reform program of Wilson, which meant that the Socialists, like the Progressives, could no longer sustain their appeal.

With the onset of World War I reform fervor was quickly replaced by a preoccupation with armament. The ability of American industry to meet the needs of the allies proved to many the inherent worth of a corporate-dominated society. The corporate leaders took advantage of this situation after the war, rolling back many of the gains won by labor before and during the war.

Labor was not the only group that suffered. The postwar "red scare," with its fear and suppression of communism, socialism, and all alien doctrines, focused on Blacks, Catholics, Jews, and immigrants.[54]

54. See Robert K. Murray, *Red Scare: A Study of National Hysteria, 1919–1920* (McGraw-Hill, 1964).

Meanwhile President Warren Harding called for a "return to normalcy." Under the leadership of Harding, Calvin Coolidge, and Herbert Hoover, normalcy reigned, with the corporate interests unchallenged in their direction of both the economic and the political policies of the nation.

The issues that had aroused the nation in the prewar years—corruption and government domination by corporate interests—were once again to command the attention of the public. But the response to them was quite different than in earlier years.

Under the Harding administration that began in 1921, the Fordney-McCumber Act reestablished extremely high tariffs. The Revenue Act of 1921, piloted through Congress by Secretary of the Treasury and multimillionaire Andrew Mellon, reduced the tax burden for the rich. Harding himself took an active antilabor position, at one point threatening to use federal troops against striking miners.

Corruption in government, a major theme of the prewar reform movement, abounded in the Harding era. The head of the Veterans Bureau, Charles R. Forbes, was early rumored to have siphoned off vast amounts of the $250 million he administered for hospitals and hospital supplies; Harding was forced to ask for his resignation in 1923. Jesse Smith, involved in the peddling of influence at the Justice Department, committed suicide shortly after his connections with the criminal world had been exposed. Teapot Dome, the most notorious scandal of Harding's years, focused on the secretary of the interior, Albert B. Fall, and his leasing of naval oil reserves in Wyoming and California to private interests. The affair involved graft and conspiracy to defraud the government, and resulted in the conviction of Fall. Never before had a cabinet officer been convicted and sentenced to prison.

As the era of normalcy began in the early 1920s, the economic recovery it depended on did not extend to the agricultural community. When their needs went unheeded by the major parties, farmers of the Northwest turned to the Nonpartisan League and the Farmer-Labor statewide parties.[55] These groups, together with urban-based reformers, formed the Conference for Progressive Political Action (CPPA) in 1922 to provide an organizational base for the many groups disenchanted with normalcy.[56] The CPPA successfully sponsored candidates for Congress and state offices in the midterm election of 1922.

With the disclosure of graft and corruption in the Harding administration, and with the Teapot Dome scandal affecting the most likely 1924 Democratic nominee for President, William G. McAdoo, the CPPA began to lay plans for a third-party campaign for 1924. Yet the organization would have preferred that one of the major parties nominate a reform candidate. Only if they failed to pull one of the major parties in their direction did they intend to use the third-party option.

THE ELECTION OF 1924

As the campaign of 1924 approached, the electorate appeared more concerned with riding the tide of urban industrial prosperity than with returning to the difficult battle required for progressive reforms. The oil scandals and corruption in the Harding administration were minimized by the timely death of the President. The popular Vice President Calvin Coolidge succeeded Harding, and the Republicans nominated him as their standard-bearer for 1924. "Keeping cool with Coolidge," the voters returned a Republican to the presidency by an overwhelming margin—54 percent of the popular vote in a three-way contest.

The only hope the CPPA had of an alliance after Coolidge's nomination was the Democrats' nomination of a reformer who would placate the neglected and angered agrarian and labor forces.

55. The Nonpartisan League, which had emerged in 1915 in North Dakota, reflected the farmers' return to belief in the necessity of direct political action. The league was most successful in its efforts to capture political power through gaining control of the Republican party machinery in primary elections. See Robert L. Morlan, *Political Prairie Fire: The Nonpartisan League, 1915–1922* (University of Minnesota Press, 1955).

56. Kenneth C. MacKay, *The Progressive Movement of 1924* (Octagon, 1966), p. 54.

Many Democrats, aware that they could not beat Coolidge without such a coalition, attempted to incorporate the CPPA. The Democratic convention, meeting in Madison Square Garden in a sweltering July heat, was torn between two competing factions. The party could adopt a reform image by nominating William McAdoo but he was tainted by the Teapot Dome scandal. It could also coalesce behind Governor Alfred E. Smith of New York, a wet, a Catholic, and a member of Tammany Hall, who had strong support among ethnic groups and industrial workers in the Northeast. Neither man, however, could capture the necessary two-thirds vote at the convention. After nine days and 103 ballots, the exhausted convention resorted to a compromise ticket with John W. Davis for President and Charles Bryan as his running mate. But the farmers rejected the compromise; Davis, a "cultivated gentleman" and an eminent corporation lawyer associated with J. P. Morgan, was an unsatisfactory candidate for them.

*The Progressive Party.* With the reform cause unrepresented in either major party, the CPPA called a convention in Cleveland in July and nominated Senator Robert M. La Follette, Sr., under the banner of a new Progressive party. Though sixty-nine years old and in poor health, La Follette accepted the call. For the vice-presidency the convention nominated Senator Burton K. Wheeler of Montana who had bolted the Democratic party when it nominated Davis. A promise of wide support was added in August when the American Federation of Labor (AFL)—the most powerful and conservative labor organization in the country—abandoned its nonpartisan tradition and openly endorsed the Progressive ticket.

While the two major-party candidates epitomized corporate interests, the Progressive party addressed the issue of corporate domination. The party's platform, echoing that a decade earlier, began with familiar themes: "The great issue before the American people today is the control of government and industry by private monopoly.... For a generation the people have struggled patiently, in the face of repeated betrayals by successive administrations, to free themselves from this intolerable power which has been undermining representative government."[57] The election revealed the minority status of the movement. By the measure of third-party voting, La Follette's 17 percent of the popular vote was significant but it was a disappointment to most Progressive leaders.

*Aftermath.* While relegated to minority status in 1924, the Progressive party offered the only alternative to corporate control, and it held the potential for future growth. Many saw it as a serious threat to the Democrats, who received only 29 percent of the vote. This threat did not materialize, for circumstance and changing Democratic leadership in 1928 returned the party system to competition between the two broadly based major parties.

The Progressive party fell into disarray immediately after the 1924 election. The AFL, which had not supported the party wholeheartedly, returned to its myriad local alliances with the major parties. When the socialists could not persuade the remaining members to organize for a permanent third-party movement, the CPPA collapsed. Hope of any future reunification between these factions ended with the death of La Follette in 1925, depriving the disparate party forces of a unifying and respected leader. Meanwhile, the Democrats had realized that in order to survive they would have to appeal to the agrarians and urban workers, providing a distinctive alternative to the Republicans. In 1928 they offered such an alternative in the candidacy of Alfred E. Smith. Although Smith was not victorious, he provided a sharp contrast to the Republican Hoover and attracted minorities and industrial workers into the Democratic party.

SIMILARITIES OF THE 1912, 1924, AND 1968 ELECTIONS

The intense national conflict over the issues of corruption in government and the regulation of corporations before and after World War I satisfies the first criterion for third-party voting. The issues were key factors in the elections of both 1912 and 1924. Beyond this point, the two elections are dissimilar.

In 1912 the electorate was split into a vast majority and two intense minorities. The majority favored a program of reforms

57. Porter and Johnson, *National Party Platforms,* p. 252.

while one sizable minority was intensely opposed and sought to preserve the status quo. A smaller minority—at the opposite end of the spectrum—demanded a complete restructuring of the political and economic system.

With the overwhelming reform sentiment in the electorate in 1912, both major parties might have been expected to advocate this position in an attempt to win the election. In fact, the Democrats did so by nominating Wilson. That the Republicans did not was the result of an atypical turn of events: for structural reasons, the faction representing reform was prevented from effectively participating in the party's convention. That faction regrouped and formed a new party that attracted a majority of the Republicans. Consequently, the second largest vote went to the new Progressive party headed by Roosevelt, and Taft was left representing the minority Old Guard Republican sentiment. The radical minority on the left, finding little comfort in the programs of the leading contenders, provided a 6 percent vote for the Socialists, their largest ever.

In 1924 the public was again split into a majority and minority on the major reformist issues. In this instance the vast majority sought normalcy, not change, and the configuration of party votes was like that in the elections of 1832, 1848, 1892, and 1968. When the two major parties responded similarly to the majority sentiment, they left unrepresented the views of an intense minority of reformers, industrial workers, and agrarians. Into this vacuum moved the Progressives, uniting behind the nationally prominent symbol of reform, "fighting" Bob La Follette.

## The Great Depression

The intense national conflict of the depression era of the 1930s was brought on by mass unemployment, outbreaks of violence, extensive labor agitation, and the growth of antidemocratic political movements on both the right and left. The controversies and conflicting pressures became increasingly bitter from 1935 onward.[58] The role of government in the economy, social legislation,

58. Dahl, *Political Oppositions*, p. 53.

aid to farmers, the power of organized labor, and many other issues were bitterly contested.

The period of conflict is unusual because the depression was so sudden and its effects so widespread and dramatic that large-scale opposition to the incumbent Republicans developed rapidly. With the stock market crash of 1929, large segments of the electorate lost faith in President Hoover's solutions to the economic crisis and opposition to his programs mushroomed. In 1932 the Democratic candidate Franklin D. Roosevelt could simply place himself in opposition to the ineffective efforts of the Republicans to revive the economy.

Although opposition to the Republican policies was widespread, it was not, at least in 1932, directed toward any ideological or radical alternative. Just as Hoover was rejected for the failures of his economic policies, so were the parties proposing a socialist, communist, or fascist restructuring of society. Even as the crisis deepened during the first Roosevelt administration, third-party impulses were contained. Roosevelt's move to the left was sufficient to incorporate most of organized labor, farmers, ethnic groups, and even many socialists in his coalition. By 1936, then, at the depth of the depression, the two major parties provided stark contrasts, with the Republicans calling for a return to the traditional free enterprise and trickle down policies, and Roosevelt pursuing a multiplicity of direct-aid governmental programs. Only the most extreme partisan found both major parties unacceptable. Consequently, no significant third-party voting developed throughout the era. In fact, the Socialist-Communist vote declined between 1932 and 1936. While many challengers loomed in the background in the 1930s, stretching from the Communist party to the Christian party, none were able to mount successful electoral campaigns.

## CRISIS WITHOUT A THIRD PARTY

In the most severe economic crisis in American history the electorate split into a majority favoring aggressive government action and a large minority favoring the status quo. Opposing positions thus became feasible election strategies for the major party contenders, and third-party contenders had no basis for a strong voter appeal.

## *The General Pattern*

Strong third parties have appeared in all but two periods of intense national conflict in the past 140 years. As different as the controversial issues, major- and third-party contenders, and alignments of voters were, significant third-party voting generally followed the same pattern. When a limited number of extremely important issues divided the electorate, creating an intense and estranged minority, the two traditional party candidates appealed to the majority. Consistently the intense minority was left angered, unrepresented, and highly susceptible to the appeals of a third party. The specific type of split that developed in 1968—the major parties equivocating though in truth adopting one position and the third party championing the position of the intense minority—is most like the three-way contests of 1832, 1848, 1892, and 1924.

The elections of 1856 and 1860 prove there is no ironclad rule that only minorities will become estranged during a period of crisis. On the contrary, divisive issues can be so great that most of the electorate divides into a number of mutually exclusive hostile camps and neither two-partyism nor the nonviolent resolution of conflict is possible.

There is always, as in 1912, the rare possibility that an entrenched leadership can thwart the obvious will of the party's constituency and prevent the nomination of a candidate who will address the burning social and political issues. If this occurs, splinter parties may well be expected, and with them significant third-party votes.

Finally, when divisive issues split the electorate evenly, or nearly so, the warring factions are usually contained within the two-party framework. The major parties, by standing apart from one another and adopting distinctive positions, in effect deny third parties their potential sources of support. This occurred in both the Reconstruction and New Deal eras.

# THIRD PARTIES IN ELECTIONS AND POLICYMAKING

SOME SCHOLARS and some politicians have berated third parties as inherently undemocratic and a threat to American political traditions. Others have characterized them as crucial components of the representative process. Similarly, the effects of third parties on public policy have sometimes been viewed as progressive and innovative, and in other instances as impediments to reasoned development of public policy. There is compelling evidence that third parties do affect the outcome of some elections and that the ideas associated with them are sometimes later reflected in public policy.[1]

## Raising Issues

Third parties dramatize and help to crystallize minority positions on issues. Unimpaired by continuing commitments or the need to seek the middle of the road, they have repeatedly forced controversies into the open, compelling the major parties to respond.

It was left to the Free Soil party, for example, to force debate on the issues of settlement and restriction of slavery in the election of 1848. The failure of the national leaders to resolve these issues led to another significant third-party showing in 1856 and

1. See Austin Ranney and Willmoore Kendall, *Democracy and the American Party System* (Harcourt, Brace, 1956), especially pt. 5.

to the emergence of two strong new contenders in the 1860 election. Three decades later the Populists brought the key concerns of western and southern farmers to national attention. The Socialist party in 1912 represented a distinctive contrast to the major parties on the controversy over the industrial system. In 1968 the pattern was repeated. Wallace was a particularly effective spokesman for a vocal white minority committed to segregation and a hard-line response to civil disobedience and street crimes; in addition, he was a champion of military victory in Vietnam.

Whether or not the positions taken by third parties seem desirable or productive, the fundamental right to voice them must be respected. In the end a democracy is protected by the reasoned choices of the electorate among all positions, not by suppression of the allegedly bad ones.

## The Contagion of Third Parties

An opposing theory holds, however, that third parties should not be accorded the same democratic protections as other parties because of their destructive potential. At issue is not a guarantee of free expression, but the threat to the stability of the democratic process inherent in third parties. The threat posed by a minority-oriented third party supposedly encourages politicians to overreact and allows extremists through the public forum provided during a campaign to incite the masses. As third parties establish themselves, they are expected to multiply, eventually locking the nation into irreconcilable conflicts behind a variety of narrowly oriented and rigid programs. The Third and Fourth French Republics, the First and Second Italian Republics, and the Weimar Republic of Germany are examples for those who fear a proliferation of political parties.

The history of the American party system does not support the notion of contagious growth of third parties. Except in the period immediately before the Civil War, nothing even close to a multiplication of third parties has occurred. And in this instance the Breckinridge Democrats and the Constitutional Union party were more manifestation than cause of the divisive conflicts that led to the collapse. In the United States the presence of one or even two significant third parties has not led to a proliferation of parties, nor to the destruction of basic democratic institutions.

## Thwarting Majority Rule

Third parties can prevent a majority of votes from going to any one of the candidates in an election. The plurality victor in such contests might not have been chosen by a majority of voters had the contest been restricted to two contenders.[2] This eventuality is unavoidable in any popular-vote system when three or more candidates compete for a single office. But have third parties, in practice, prevented majority elections, or denied victory to the most preferred of the two major-party candidates? Is it possible, without eliminating all but two contenders, to arrive at a viable scheme for achieving majority rule? Finally, is a dogmatic principle of majority rule desirable in presidential elections?

The question whether third parties have prevented majorities from forming as well as denying victory to one of the major parties actually divides into a question of the contest for popular votes and another of the contest in the electoral college. The answer to the latter question is an emphatic no. In all elections with significant third-party votes, one of the major parties has carried a majority of the electoral college. Never has a third party either played the role of kingmaker in the electoral college by throwing its votes to one of the major parties or forced a contingent election in the House of Representatives.

However, third parties have prevented the formation of popular majorities on a number of occasions, and have also affected the

2. This is always a possibility in a three (or more) party election. For instance, if three candidates receive 40 percent, 45 percent, and 15 percent, respectively, of the vote, in most American elections the candidate with 45 percent would be declared the victor. But if the third party had been excluded from the ballot, its supporters might have given their votes to the second runner who would then have been the winner. In effect, when second preferences are considered, the most preferred candidate may be thwarted in the three-way contest.

outcome of elections by drawing off popular votes disproportionately from one of the major parties, leaving victory to the other.
In a number of those presidential elections, restricting competition
to the two traditional parties might have produced different outcomes. Of course, in the three-way contests of 1832 and 1924, the
elections were carried by more than 50 percent of the popular
vote; the majority's preferred candidate did win. The final outcome of the three-party contests of 1848, 1856, 1860, 1892, 1912,
and 1968 might have been changed by eliminating the third parties,
for the victors won by pluralities.

Whether these elections failed to go to the most preferred candidate, as determined by a majority vote in a two-way contest, is a
far more difficult question to answer. There is no conclusive evidence as to voters' subordinate preferences among the candidates,
since only their first choice is indicated by the actual vote. The
strategies of the major parties might have been different, had there
been no third party. Moreover, popular votes are filtered through
the electoral college, which reflects shifts in state choices and only
indirectly in the national vote, thus compounding the problem.

Some evidence does exist on the second preference of third-party
voters in the 1968 election—their choice in a two-party contest—
and for other elections, plausible estimates can be ventured. In a
few cases, ambiguities prevent even tentative speculation about the
extent to which restricting the election to the two traditional
parties would have changed the outcome. A key assumption underlying the speculation about alternative outcomes is that dramatic
shifts in the proportion of popular votes that would result from the
removal of the third party would also cause shifts in the electoral
college and thus in the outcome of the election.

EXCLUDING THIRD-PARTY CONTENDERS

Most pundits believe that the less than 1 percentage point lead
of Richard Nixon over Hubert Humphrey in the 1968 election
would have widened appreciably, to the point of a majority victory
for Nixon, had the third-party contender's name been withheld

from the ballot and the Wallace voters' second preferences been used to determine the outcome.

The election survey of the Survey Research Center (SRC) at the University of Michigan indicated that although more Wallace voters were Democrats than Republicans, Nixon was preferred over Humphrey by Wallace supporters by 5 to 4.[3] These findings are consistent with other findings that Wallace supporters were drawn more by issues than traditional party ties, and that while only a second choice, Nixon was closer to their views on the crucial issues than was Humphrey. Moreover, throughout the 1950s and early 1960s many southern Democrats had voted the party label in state and local elections while voting Republican in presidential contests. Thus, finding that Wallace-voting Democratic partisans supported the Republican nominee as their second choice is not surprising. Hence, the SRC analysts find it "difficult to maintain any suspicion that the Wallace intrusion by itself changed the major outcome of the election."[4]

In mid-October a national survey found that Wallace supporters overwhelmingly favored Nixon when forced to decide between the two major-party candidates; 58 percent chose Nixon and 22 percent Humphrey, 14 percent responded "won't vote," and 6 percent were "not sure."[5] Again, in a simulated rerun of the election, where votes were determined from a scale of candidate preferences and with Wallace removed as a possible choice, Nixon emerged with 55 percent of the popular vote, carrying 60 percent of the white population. In the shift, 73 percent of the Wallace leaners moved to Nixon.[6]

Further back in history, the 1856 presidential election was also carried by a plurality, but as in 1968 the plurality winner, James

3. Philip E. Converse and others, "Continuity and Change in American Politics: Parties and Issues in the 1968 Election," *American Political Science Review*, vol. 63 (December 1969), table 3, p. 1091.

4. Ibid., p. 1092.

5. Response to NBC-Quayle survey 1176, a special report by Oliver Quayle and Company to the National Broadcasting Company's News Election Unit; reported in Karl Boughan, "The Wallace Phenomenon: Racist Populism and American Electoral Politics" (Ph.D. thesis, Harvard University, 1971), p. 422.

6. Ibid., p. 423.

Buchanan, probably would have won even if the third contender, the American party, had been dropped from the ballot. Although a coalition of the American party and the second-place Republican party would have produced a majority, the two parties' views on slavery restriction make such an alliance highly improbable. More likely, the American party's constituency in the South would have chosen the Democratic column or sat out the election, a shift to the restrictionist Republicans being unthinkable. The party's northern constituency might or might not have moved to the Democratic party. If only the American party's southern constituency were with him, however, Buchanan would still have been the overwhelming victor, carrying the nation with more than 57 percent of the popular vote in a two-way contest with John Frémont. Thus the plurality victor on first preferences was also the most likely majority victor when the most plausible second preference of third-party voters is considered.

The election contest in 1912 was far too complex to justify speculation on the consequences of removing the third-party contenders. Obviously, the Republicans if unified behind a single candidate could have carried the election with well over a majority of the votes; the party's presidential vote went from 52 percent in 1908 to a combined Roosevelt-Taft vote of 57 percent in 1912. But the extraordinary characteristic of the election was the division in the Republican ranks. Thus, even if Taft is cast as the party's nominee in a contest with Wilson, there is little way of knowing what the second preference of Roosevelt's supporters would have been. It is equally difficult to determine where the Socialists would have turned if Debs had been barred from the contest.

The election of 1892 is as hard to decipher. In the three preceding elections the Democrats and Republicans had received almost identical portions of the popular vote, with the runner-up always within 1 percentage point of the victor. Moreover, since the major-party candidates of 1892 were the same as in 1888—Grover Cleveland for the Democrats and Benjamin Harrison for the Republicans—the exclusion of the Populist ticket would in all likelihood have resulted in another very close contest. Whether the second preferences of Populist voters might have reversed the outcome is impossible to gauge.

An election where the absence of third parties would likely have changed the outcome—the victor would not have won a majority determined from the second choice of third-party voters—is that of 1860. The four-way contest in the election makes speculation about probable outcomes somewhat complicated. However, the South could only have turned to the Democrat in choosing between the nominees of the traditional major parties. With the Constitutional Union party and the Breckinridge Democrats removed, southerners would undoubtedly have chosen Douglas, if only to prevent the victory of the slavery restrictionist Republicans, represented by Lincoln. Although some of the Constitutional Union constituency in the border states and the North could be expected to shift to the Republican column, Lincoln could have bettered his 40 percent popular vote very little, whereas Douglas, with the South behind him, would have swept the nation. Hence, Lincoln, the plurality victor in the four-party contest of 1860, would not have been the victor in a two-way contest restricted to the major parties.

Removing the third-party candidate and relying on second preferences of his supporters would probably have changed the outcome in 1848 as well. The victory of the Whig candidate, Zachary Taylor, depended on the division of the Democratic vote in the North on the restriction of slavery between the party's nominee, Lewis Cass, and the third-party Free Soil challenger, Martin Van Buren. With Van Buren out of the contest, Cass would probably have won.

Throughout the era the Democrats were the dominant presidential party, winning in 1844 and again in 1852 after the Whig upset of 1848. Moreover, the Free Soil candidate was a Democratic defector who led many New Yorkers as well as the abolitionist faction out of the party in 1848. The Free Soil vote, though drawn from Whig, Democratic, and Liberty factions, came disproportionately from the traditional Democratic constituencies of the North.[7]

In general, whenever the third-party vote in a presidential election has been significant, majority rule—in the sense of one candidate receiving more than 50 percent of the popular votes—has been abridged. But removing the third-party contender would in all probability have changed the outcome of the election in only a very few instances. There may be methods of selection, however, that would assure majority victories in all elections, without resorting to the arbitrary and undemocratic practice of eliminating all but the two traditional parties.

### ALTERNATIVE VOTING SCHEMES

A number of alternatives to the present system would arrive at majority decisions in multiparty contests by considering voter preferences. In a runoff system all parties are allowed to enter the first election. If none receives a majority vote, a second election is held between the two leading contenders.

A major, practical drawback to this scheme is the extra time and money required for runoffs. Consequently, they have never been widely favored among American politicians. A more subtle problem is the possibility that the runoff victor will not in fact be the most preferred candidate—although the system guarantees a majority winner in the second election. The candidate who placed third, fourth, or further down the line in the initial election could conceivably have been the second choice of a majority of voters, but the runoff is restricted to first-preference contestants. The winner in the runoff may be preferred over his second-round opponent, but not over one of the excluded contenders. It is questionable whether the system is a more democratic method of selection than the current one. A better method would take the preference orderings of voters across all candidates into consideration.

The Condorcet voting scheme, designed to select the most preferred candidate, requires voters to rank each candidate against each other candidate. The candidate who defeats each of the others

7. Joseph G. Rayback, *Free Soil: The Election of 1848* (University Press of Kentucky, 1970), p. 299.

in these one-on-one contests "can be taken as standing higher than the others on voters' schedules of preference,"[8] and is declared the winner. The scheme makes it possible to abide by majority rule without restricting the contest to two parties. Had this method of selection been applied to the four-way contest of 1912, the Roosevelt Progressive party might have emerged victor. Wilson, the actual victor, would most likely have won easily in his pairings against Taft and Debs, as would Roosevelt against those two. The outcome would have hinged on the pairing between Wilson and Roosevelt. The conservative Republicans, having no better refuge in this contest, would probably have backed Roosevelt, thus making him the most preferred of all candidates. This strongly suggests that at least in some instances the elimination of third parties may deny, rather than making easier, the selection of the most preferred candidate.

The main drawback of the pairing method of selection is the possibility that it will produce a voting paradox. Individual preference orderings may be assumed to be transitive, the preference over one candidate including the preference of that candidate over another. The group decision, however, may be intransitive. Thus, in a three-way contest, it is conceivable that each of the candidates will be preferred over another, leaving unresolved the question of which candidate is to be declared the victor.[9]

Another scheme of preference orderings avoids that problem. Voters rank all candidates, assigning point scores to each in descending order. The candidate who accumulates the greatest number of points across the electorate is the victor. But even this seemingly straightforward scheme has shortcomings. For instance, what relative weights should be assigned to first, second, and succeeding preferences? If the lowest-ranking candidate is assigned a score of 0, the next 1, and so on up,[10] the candidate who wins an

---

8. Duncan Black, *The Theory of Committees and Elections* (Cambridge University Press, 1963), p. 57.

9. Kenneth J. Arrow, *Social Choice and Individual Value*, Cowles Foundation Monograph 12 (2nd ed., Wiley, 1963), pp. 13–14.

10. This method of weighting was chosen as the most logical by Jean Charles de Borda, who originated the weighting scheme. See Black, *Theory of Committees and Elections*, pp. 59–66.

absolute majority of first preference votes, as well as a majority against each of the other contenders, could still lose the election based on total point scores. The serious flaw in this method is the incentive it provides voters to misrepresent their true preference orderings in order to advance the cause of their most preferred candidate.[11]

In short, while runoffs, pairwise orderings, and ranking schemes all avoid the problem of abridging majority rule in multiparty elections, each is plagued with its own serious problems. Runoffs are not designed to select the most preferred candidate; paired preferences may paradoxically fail to turn up a group preference; and ranked preferences raise not only theoretical questions of weighting but also problems of how to prevent voters from distorting their true orderings. Hence, the only feasible means of assuring that the presidential selection is by a popular majority, as opposed to a plurality, is to restrict the contest to two contestants. However, restricting access to the electoral arena means, in actuality, guaranteeing a monopoly to the two existing parties. And denying third parties the right to participate may in itself prevent the election of the most preferred candidate based on second-order preferences.

The important role played by third parties in raising issues and keeping the system responsive to demands of diverse groups in the electorate does not seem to be outweighed by the violation of majority rule that can occur when third parties receive an appreciable number of votes. This has apparently been the consensus at many other election levels; winning by less than an absolute majority of first-preference votes—where plurality rules prevail—is considered quite democratic in thousands of state and local election districts across the nation. Consequently, in spite of the sacrosanct position majority rule holds in the rhetoric of democratic theory, in fact it has rarely been adhered to. And it is an unconvincing justification for the suppression of third parties.

11. For an explanation of these methods and a discussion of their shortcomings, see Max S. Power, "Logic and Legitimacy: On Understanding the Electoral College Controversy," in Donald R. Matthews, ed., *Perspectives on Presidential Selection* (Brookings Institution, 1973), pp. 204–37.

## Extending the Electoral Base

Third parties, it is argued, expand the base of electoral politics. By appealing to constituencies uninvolved in politics and largely ignored by the major parties, they add relevance to an election for numerous Americans. The Wallace campaign of 1968, for example, appears to have activated a fair portion of America's usually inactive rural population. Wallace's constituency was located disproportionately in communities of less than 10,000 persons among those of rural origin, little involved in elective politics and mistrustful of the government and the political institutions of the nation.[12]

Overall voter participation in three-party contests does not normally reflect such increased interest. In six of the eight elections where one or more third parties provided a significant challenge to the two major parties—1832, 1848, 1892, 1912, 1924, and 1968 —the level of participation by eligible voters declined. Only in the two extremely divisive pre-Civil War contests of 1856 and 1860 did participation increase.[13]

### INTEREST UP, VOTING DOWN

Although third parties may activate some voters, the overall level of voter participation across the nation declines when they appear. An important clue to the change is George Wallace's often repeated theme: "There ain't a dime's worth of difference between the Democratic and Republican parties." Wallace is not alone in his view; less than half the electorate, according to SRC studies, saw any important difference between the Democrats and Repub-

12. James McEvoy III, *Radicals or Conservatives? The Contemporary American Right* (Rand McNally, 1971), pp. 116–26. See also Walter Dean Burnham, "Political Immunization and Political Confessionalism: Some Comparative Inquiries" (paper prepared for delivery at the 8th world congress of the International Political Science Association, 1970).

13. See U.S. Bureau of the Census, *Historical Statistics of the Untied States, Colonial Times to 1957* (1960), table 427-31; and Congressional Quarterly Service, *Politics in America* (3rd ed., Congressional Quarterly Service, 1969), pp. 124–27.

licans throughout the 1950s and 1960s.[14] This tweedledum-tweedle-dee characterization of the major parties applied in a number of important policy areas. Just preceding the 1968 election 47 percent of the SRC poll respondents identified foreign affairs (presumably Vietnam) as the most important problem facing the nation; 28 percent identified race relations and public order.[15] Almost four-fifths of the respondents were "very much" or "somewhat" interested in the 1968 campaign, the highest level of interest in an election recorded by the SRC since 1952.[16] Meanwhile, on the leading issues the electorate considered the only real alternative to be between Wallace and both of the major-party standard-bearers, Nixon and Humphrey.

This is not surprising. When the electorate splits into a large majority and an intense minority, major-party candidates have little flexibility in establishing their positions if they seriously intend to win. Because of the overriding importance of one or two issues, it becomes politically impossible for them to advocate the minority position. Third parties are the beneficiaries of this neglect. Their positions are all the more obvious because of the similarity between the major parties. Yet with little chance of a third-party victory, many persons not holding the minority view have little incentive to vote.[17]

14. Response to the question asked in 1952, 1960, and 1968, "Do you think there are any important differences in what the Republicans and Democrats stand for?" (wording changed slightly across the surveys). University of Michigan, Survey Research Center (SRC), "The 1952 American Election Study" (rev. ed., Ann Arbor: Inter-University Consortium for Political Research, 1971; processed); and Election Studies for 1960 and 1968 (rev. eds., 1970 and 1971). The major parties nevertheless appear distinctively different on some issues in some years. See Gerald Pomper, "From Confusion to Clarity: Issues and American Voters, 1956–1968," *American Political Science Review*, vol. 66 (June 1972), pp. 415–28.

15. See Chapter 1, note 17, p. 6.

16. Response to the election survey question repeated from 1952 to 1968: "Some people don't pay much attention to political campaigns. How about you, would you say that you have been very much interested, somewhat interested, or not much interested in following the political campaigns this year?" SRC, Election Studies for 1952, 1956 (rev. ed., 1968), 1960, 1964 (rev. ed., 1971), and 1968.

17. The conclusion, although somewhat speculative, is consistent with two key variables in the voting calculus developed by William H. Riker and Peter C. Ordeshook: "the differential benefit...that an individual voter receives from the success of his more preferred candidate over his less preferred one" (do you care

In addition, the third-party candidate is seldom viewed as a likely winner in the election. On the eve of the 1968 election only 5 percent of the SRC's respondents thought Wallace would win, whereas 79 percent predicted victory for either Nixon or Humphrey, and 16 percent were uncertain.[18] With the minority position highly visible, with little expectation of a third-party victory, and with the victory for the majority position (be it Democratic or Republican) assured, only 56 percent of the respondents "cared very much" or "cared pretty much" which party won the presidency. The level of concern represents a 14 percentage point decline from that in the previous election, the greatest decline recorded in the SRC studies of elections.[19] Many adherents to the majority position evidently did not see either anything unique enough about one of the major candidates to prompt them to care which would win or a great enough electoral threat in Wallace to cause them to vote.[20]

In years of a strong third-party endeavor the major parties have little incentive to conduct extensive registration or voter-turnout drives. Yet these are the major mechanisms for bringing large num-

---

who wins?) and "the probability that the citizen will, by voting, bring about the benefit" (how likely is it that the candidate or candidates favored require your vote for victory?). In 1968, according to their formula, the expected utility of a vote cast for either major-party candidate would vary little in its effect on the leading issues, and would be almost unnecessary as a contribution to the defeat of Wallace. Therefore, a decline in turnout would be expected. See "A Theory of the Calculus of Voting," *American Political Science Review*, vol. 62 (March 1968), pp. 25–42.

18. Based on responses to the question, "Who do you think will be elected President in November?" SRC, Election Study for 1968.

19. Response to the election survey question repeated from 1952 to 1968, "Generally speaking, would you say that you personally care a good deal which party wins the presidential election this fall or that you don't care very much which party wins?" Ibid.; and Election Studies for 1952, 1956, 1960, and 1964.

20. The decline in turnout has also been ascribed to cross-pressures. When an individual has equally strong inclinations toward two or more of the contestants, the dissonance is resolved by withdrawal—by losing interest in the contest and staying home on election day. See Seymour M. Lipset and others, "The Psychology of Voting," in Gardner Lindzey, ed., *Handbook of Social Psychology*, vol. 2 (Addison-Wesley, 1954), especially pp. 1133–34. Quite likely, some degree of cross-pressure exists in every election, and with a new party in the field, old attachments will surely be strained. From survey data the election of 1968 appears to have been one of an appreciable rise in interest in the contest, not one of a widespread decline in interest and thus withdrawal characteristic of massive cross-pressures.

bers of new voters to the polls. A widespread effort to register or turn out voters is likely when one of the major parties can expect to benefit disproportionately, a position the Democrats have been in at least since the New Deal. Nonvoters are disproportionately of lower socioeconomic status, a class the Democratic party has championed, and registration drives have brought in more Democratic partisans than Republican.

But who could expect to benefit from an extensive recruitment drive in 1968? For the Republicans the best strategy was to sway traditionally Democratic supporters already in the active electorate, a strategy they appear to have followed. The Democrats might have followed their usual strategy of recruiting among the pool of nonvoters. However, even if the resources had been available for such a drive, could the leaders have been confident that they would gain advantage in votes? Not likely. It was Wallace who had a disproportionately high following among the nonvoting rural and poor whites, and throughout the blue-collar class.[21] Consequently, neither the Democratic party nor its ally, organized labor, could confidently recruit large numbers of nonvoters in anticipation of a partisan gain. At best, they could appeal to their traditional supporters, hoping that partisan ties would prevail over Wallace's appeal. The third-party contender was so preoccupied with establishing his party nationally, and his organizational resources were so limited, that Wallace appears to have been unable effectively to mount a voter registration or turnout drive.

These same factors were at play in most of the preceding elections contested by significant third parties. In only two instances did the proportion of eligible voters who turned out increase rather than decrease. In these instances, front-runners offered quite different positions. In 1856 the issue of slavery had divided the country into three very distinct camps: the Republicans appealed to one group demanding exclusion of slavery from the territories, the Democratic candidate equivocated on the issue, and the American party was the recipient of the proslavery votes. The electorate was provided three choices, not similar positions by the leading two

21. See McEvoy, *Radicals or Conservatives?* chap. 5.

candidates. Concern about the outcome of the election ran high, and the level of participation increased. The same situation, but more exaggerated, existed in 1860. The positions taken on slavery in the territories by the four parties in 1860 were all different and generated widespread interest. Again, in this exceptional case, the number of voters participating in the election increased.

## Program Implementation

The fact that third parties dramatize positions on issues in an election campaign does not mean that their positions are forthwith made the cornerstones of public policy. Immigration was not halted in the 1850s in response to the demands of the nativist American party, nor were the railroad, telegraph, and telephone industries nationalized following the showing of the Populist party in 1892. The Coolidge and Hoover administrations did not make the sweeping reforms in the industrial system called for by the 1924 Progressives. After decades of campaigning, the Socialist party has yet to achieve its essential objectives.

Although third parties' programs may not be implemented directly or immediately, many of their ideas have eventually been incorporated into the programs of major parties and translated into public policies. The slavery restriction and internal improvement themes of the Free Soil party of 1848 and 1852 were seized by the Republican party in 1856, and both became public policy under the Republican administrations of the 1860s. Progressive taxation, regulation of railroads, child labor laws, and social insurance were ideas introduced into the political dialogue by Socialists, Farmer-Laborites, Progressives, and Populists. The major portion of the New Deal programs of Franklin Roosevelt are in some quarters attributed to the Progressive platforms of the preceding decades.[22]

Third parties have been particularly prominent in battles over suffrage and election reform. Long before such ideas were accepted by the major parties, the Populists, Progressives, and Socialists were

22. See Kenneth C. MacKay, *The Progressive Movement of 1924* (Octagon, 1966).

advocating the direct election of U.S. senators, women's suffrage, the recall and referendum, primary elections, and corrupt practice legislation, most of which were enacted in the late nineteenth and early twentieth centuries. On most of these issues, however, the connection between third-party activity and the adoption of programs is neither direct nor pervasive. Like most third-party programs, their adoption depended on factors often beyond the control of a minority party.

### POLICY IMPACT OF THE POPULIST PARTY

Intervening events are often responsible for the adoption of programs initially supported by third parties. The Populist demands of 1892, the expression of southern and western outrage against eastern domination of the monetary and transportation systems, were aimed at wresting control from private interests and placing it in the hands of a popularly elected national government. The party's platform called for the creation of a national currency issued only by the federal government, "without the use of banking corporations"—that is, the large banking firms of the East such as the House of Morgan. The party advocated the "unlimited coinage of silver and gold," viewing opposition to this means of immediately expanding the money supply as part of eastern banking interests' unceasing efforts to keep farmers in a state of debt and deprivation.

After the election of 1892 the currency supply did expand, and prosperity returned. Eventually, Congress provided the types of direct national aid desired by the Populists through programs that allowed farmers to borrow money against farm products (Warehouse Act of 1916); established farm loan banks (1916) and intermediate credit banks (1923); established a postal savings system (1911); and provided support for farm prices and purchase of surpluses (Federal Farm Board, 1929, Commodity Credit Corporation, 1933, Agricultural Adjustment Administration, 1933, 1938).[23]

But the agitation and enthusiasm of the Populist party influenced these developments only in the most indirect fashion. The

23. Murray S. Stedman and Susan W. Stedman, *Discontent at the Polls* (Columbia University Press, 1950), p. 21.

expansion of the supply of money was certainly not brought about by Populist demands. The party's programs were resoundingly defeated during both the Cleveland and the McKinley administrations (the silver plank was, however, adopted by the Democratic nominee, William Jennings Bryan, in his 1896 campaign). The response to the "free coinage of silver" demand was the repeal in 1893 of the purchase clause of the Sherman Silver Purchase Act.[24] This eliminated even the minimal federal subsidization of the silver industry as well as any efforts to expand currency through coinage of silver that had been in effect before the Populist party appeared in strength. In 1900 the United States converted to a single gold standard with passage of the Gold Standard Act. The demand for the nationalization of banking was also long ignored, being only partially recognized in the Federal Reserve Act of 1914. Even then, the regulations had little to do with the needs of farmers, and it is hard to see them as an accomplishment of the Populist party. The banking interests of the East that were anathema to the Populists had sought the legislation in order to consolidate their cartel-like control of the monetary system.[25] Through it they gained almost complete authority to establish and direct national monetary policy. Only indirectly, if at all, did the Federal Reserve Act result in better banking services for the agricultural community of the South and West.

Nor was the farm legislation passed after 1910 a result of Populist efforts. The early lobbying by the Farmers' Education and Cooperative Union of the South and the American Society of Equity of the West was followed by the extremely powerful efforts of the Farm Bureau Federation and the influential National Farmers' Union.[26] These organizations, which arose in the twentieth century to meet the special economic and political needs of farmers, provided effective alternatives to the seeming futility of the third-party

24. Milton Friedman and Anna Jacobson Schwartz, *A Monetary History of the United States 1867–1960* (Princeton University Press, 1963), p. 116.

25. See Gabriel Kolko, *The Triumph of Conservatism* (Quadrangle, 1967), chap. 10.

26. See Grant McConnell, *The Decline of Agrarian Democracy* (University of California Press, 1953).

strategy attempted in the 1890s. The Farmers' Education and Co-operative Union drew on the political experiences of the Grange and Alliance farm organizations that had collapsed under the stress of direct participation in electoral politics.[27] The Union leadership refused to enter partisan politics, but at both the state and national levels the organization conducted intensive lobbying campaigns. In this instance the Populist party served only as an example of how not to proceed.

The farm programs of the twentieth century were not Populist party ideas that through an evolutionary process were incorporated into public law two and three decades later. Rather they were most often the design of lobbyists who worked with major-party office-holders in the national government, far beyond the scrutiny of the general public and seldom to the advantage of the poor small farm-ers of the Populist constituency. While this legislation aided some farmers, it was neither the subtreasury plan nor the nationalization program at the heart of the third-party proposals of the earlier era. In fact, the Populists "never won their demand for federal owner-ship and management of railroads and telephone and telegraph sys-tems, or for free silver and a policy of managed inflation. Contrary to the Populists' (and others') demands, the maintenance of large standing armies of industrial mercenaries reached new heights dur-ing the Progressive Era; so too did national aid to private corpora-tions for a variety of purposes."[28]

The relief that did come to farmers in the late 1890s was brought on by a series of crop failures in Europe that boosted demand for American farm produce, and the large influx of gold into the world currency market came from fresh discoveries in South Africa, Alaska, and Colorado.[29] The increases in farm prices and available cash accompanied accelerating demands for farm products from the expanding urban industrial markets at home and abroad that

27. See Carl C. Taylor, *The Farmers' Movement 1620–1920* (American Book, 1953), pp. 359–603.
28. R. M. Abrams, ed., *Issues of the Populist and Progressive Eras, 1892–1912* (Harper and Row, 1969), p. 46.
29. Friedman and Schwartz, *Monetary History*, p. 9.

helped extend the newfound prosperity well into the twentieth century.

POLICY IMPACT OF THE AIP

Unlike the Populist party, the American Independent party has generally been credited with success in having its programs adopted. Critics have accused the Nixon administration of over-reacting to the Wallace sentiment and forsaking the nation's commitment to full realization of a racially integrated society. Since the early days of the administration, school integration has been the principal point at issue. Attempts to appease southern congressmen led by Senator Strom Thurmond, Republican of South Carolina and staunch Nixon supporter in the 1968 campaign, led to postponement in 1969 and 1970 of deadlines in the school desegregation plans of the Department of Health, Education, and Welfare.[30] Southern school officials interpreted the slowdown as a withdrawal of pressure to desegregate. Where desegregation plans were actually implemented, black principals and faculty were often demoted or fired, and the federal government failed to intervene.[31] For the first time, the Justice Department sided with school districts, both North and South, against civil rights plantiffs.

Finally, in March of 1972, the President in a televised address to the nation called for a reexamination of all busing proposals to determine whether they were unduly demanding. Blaming the wave of reaction against busing on overzealous lower court rulings, the President questioned the federal courts' authority to move against de facto segregation or to require busing as a remedy to segregation in any but the most extreme cases. Nixon appeared to have adopted the segregationists' reasoning that the posture of the courts, not the existence of segregation and racial animosities, was

30. See Leon E. Panetta and Peter Gall, *Bring Us Together: The Nixon Team and the Civil Rights Retreat* (Lippincott, 1971).

31. Samuel B. Ethridge, assistant executive secretary of the National Education Association, estimated that by mid-1971 more than 1,000 black principals and 5,000 teachers had lost their jobs. See Charles Rabb, "HEW, Justice lawyers draft plan to implement Supreme Court's busing decision," *National Journal*, June 19, 1971, p. 1312.

splitting the country. He then sent to Congress an equal educational opportunities bill and a student transportation moratorium bill designed to deal with the problems.

These relaxations of the moral and legal pressure on the South, and the nation, to integrate racially certainly served to placate Wallace's constituency. Yet the major policies that had been articulated by Wallace—repeal of the civil rights acts of the 1960s and a return to local control over school integration policies ("freedom of choice")—were not enacted under Nixon. In fact, changing events probably had far more to do with Nixon's strong actions against massive school integration than the threat of George Wallace and his constituency. Only when desegregation became a live issue for a very broad segment of the population did Nixon take dramatic and decisive steps.

Until 1972 Nixon held off committing himself publicly to permanent relief for those opposing school desegregation. And this came only after a federal district judge had ordered the merger of the Richmond city schools with the white suburban schools in the adjacent county. Meanwhile, another judge directly assaulted the North, ruling that the de jure segregation in the Detroit school system was the result of official government action and might be rectified only by extending the system to the entire Detroit metropolitan area. Metropolitanwide integration plans, in Detroit or elsewhere, raised the specter of racial conflicts like those that had occurred in Pontiac, Michigan, in 1971.

These court decisions brought an immediate reaction from whites throughout the nation. With poll respondents' opposition to busing (to achieve school integration) increasing from 41 percent in 1971 to 69 percent in 1972,[32] and with the courts moving on Nixon's most cherished constituency, suburban whites, the President moved in to promise immediate and effective action; busing would be halted.

True, AIP supporters would benefit from this policy wherever de facto segregation was under legal attack, but Nixon made no mention of returning to the dual school systems of the South.

32. Harris Survey Report, *Washington Post*, April 10, 1972.

George Wallace, for one, did not lose sight of the thrust of the Nixon proposal. While pleased to see the President coming out against busing, he believed, as he told a convention of Alabama educators, that Nixon should go even further and rectify the injustice already imposed on the South by instructing the Justice Department to reopen all schools under a freedom-of-choice plan.

Although Nixon moved decisively in the AIP direction, he did so only when a much larger segment of the population than those who voted for Wallace in 1968 came to agree with its views. George Wallace, both as spokesman for the AIP constituency and as political rival, might have prompted Nixon to take stronger action than he would otherwise have chosen; but the President did not adopt Wallace's anti-civil-rights-acts and freedom-of-choice plans.

## *Third Parties in the Policymaking Process*

The role of third parties in the policymaking process can vary, depending on how public opinion moves. Third parties usually champion what at least at the outset are minority views. Those views must await broader public acceptance before their adoption by the major parties that translate public demands into policy. But adoption of a third party's views by a broader public does not guarantee adoption of its programs by the major parties. Officeholders can be quite selective in deciding which aspects of a third party's program they will implement in response to rising public demand. The ideas that the major parties fail to accept either come to rest with fringe parties or fade back into the general reservoir of public opinions.

☆

*Chapter Four*

☆

# CONSTRAINTS ON THIRD PARTIES

THIRD PARTIES in national elections invariably face an uphill battle. Such powerful forces as the election of a single chief executive support the formation of only two competing parties. In addition, the major parties sometimes use their power as lawmakers and administrators to exclude additional contenders.

Laws governing candidates' access to the ballot can be especially inequitable. Filing requirements, for example, are often designed to maintain the position of the two preeminent parties. Similarly, petition laws may require new parties to collect ridiculously large numbers of signatures in order to be placed on the ballot.

Such election laws often impede third parties. Whether they prevent third parties from competing is a different matter. Public awareness that ballot laws are especially difficult barriers for third parties proved an asset in George Wallace's 1968 campaign. In qualifying for the ballot in California, an almost impossible feat, Wallace won both publicity and credibility. The flow of funds into his campaign headquarters also increased. Indeed, Wallace's achievement in California made the American Independent party (AIP) a national movement that could not be ignored.

An extremely important ingredient of modern electoral politics is television campaigning. Equal access to the mass media is guaranteed to all political parties by Section 315(a) of the Communications Act of 1934. But Section 315(a) was weakened by amendment in 1959; it was suspended entirely for the 1960 presidential election; and current legislative proposals would eliminate it altogether. The structure of laws governing the use of mass media is crucial to any political party, but especially new and smaller ones. Denial of equal or proportionate air time for these parties may prove to be a paramount factor in their future.

A reform proposal closely related to third-party activity is replacement of the electoral college presidential election by a direct popular vote. It is often argued that a proliferation of third parties would follow a shift to direct popular vote. That may not be the case.

## Access to the Ballot

If election laws explicitly denied access to the ballot to all but the Democratic and Republican parties, their partisan bias would be obvious, and their repeal would probably be a burning issue. In fact, maintenance of the two reigning parties has rarely been their aim. Rather, they have been designed either to eliminate corrupt election practices or to reduce voters' choices to a reasonable number. Voters are assumed to be unable to make a reasoned and sound judgment on election day with hundreds or even dozens of candidates on the ballot. Not only would a long list of candidates cause confusion, but in all probability elections would be carried by very small pluralities—as a general rule, the larger the field of contestants, the smaller the number of votes needed to win. Thus, filing dates, petitions, loyalty oaths, and so forth, are required by many states.

Lawmakers and administrators do have an obligation to keep the number of contenders within tolerable limits. But what is tolerable? Are three, four, seven, eight, or even more candidates acceptable, or is it in the general interest to define the manageable and desirable number as two? Moreover, to what extent are constitutional rights jeopardized when, as has often been the case, election laws place extraordinary burdens in the paths of smaller and new parties?

Historically the mandate of the government to administer elections had little to do with limiting the number of political parties.

Before the Civil War the conduct of elections was largely left to the political parties themselves. Any group that wanted to compete for office could do so by printing and distributing its own ballot. The growth of corrupt political machines after the war precipitated widespread demands for nonpartisan and publicly administered elections. The response was adoption of the secret ballot—what was known as the Australian ballot—at the turn of the century.[1] The government assumed sole authority for financing, printing, and furnishing the ballot. Henceforth, only the official state ballot was valid; the procedures for nominating candidates were regulated by law; ballots were to be marked in secret; and violators of the law were subject to criminal prosecution. At its inception the secret ballot was hailed as a triumph over corrupt politicians. It was, on the whole, a cure for the rampant fraud, intimidation, coercion, ballot-box stuffing, and flagrant disregard for the right of every person to vote his preference freely.[2]

The negative effects of governmental administration of elections were not so obvious at the outset. They are rooted in the fact that government officials are not only agents of the state, but also partisan politicians. Thus the Democrats and Republicans have been able to use the authority of the state indirectly to handicap if not eliminate the opposition.

THE PENDULUM SWINGS

Under the early forms of the Australian ballot, third parties and independent candidates could, with relative ease, qualify for a position. Before the First World War, petition was the most common method of getting on the ballot; it was used in all but four states.[3]

---

1. Charles E. Merriam and Harold F. Gosnell, *The American Party System* (3rd ed., Macmillan, 1940), pp. 388–93.

2. The procedural reforms of the progressive era, making the government an active participant in the electoral process, have not universally been seen as a blessing. It has been argued that "most if not all of these fundamental changes in the 'rules of the game' were in effect devices of political stabilization and control, with strongly conservative latent consequences if not overt justifications." Walter Dean Burnham, *Critical Elections and the Mainsprings of American Politics* (Norton, 1970), p. 74.

3. Eldon C. Evans, *A History of the Australian Ballot System in the United States* (University of Chicago Press, 1917), p. 31.

The required number of signatures varied from 50 in Mississippi to 10 percent of the total votes cast in the previous general election in Nevada. As a rule the requirement was around 1 or 2 percent of the vote.

Filing deadlines, which served only to facilitate efficient elections, were usually reasonable. Connecticut, for instance, required that parties nominate candidates three weeks prior to the day of election; in some states the deadline fell even closer to the election. Generally, filing dates left officials enough time to print the ballot, while allowing new parties or factions dissatisfied with the nominees selected at the state or national conventions of the major parties to enter candidates.

The public, courts, and state officials apparently interpreted the mandate under the Australian ballot laws to be one of conducting expedient and honest elections—nothing more, nothing less. Qualification for ballot position was based primarily on a minimum demonstration of support, and on the need for time to print ballots and to publicize a list of contenders. Within a very few years these laws underwent a number of changes that are difficult to justify as furthering the government's mandate to conduct efficient and honest elections.

By 1924 the Progressive party found state laws "almost insuperable obstacles to a new party."[4] Access to the ballot was not a problem in states like Georgia and Virginia, where only notification of candidacy was required. In Tennessee the task was accomplished with the aid of only 15 signatures. In other states, however, the La Follette ticket was placed on the ballot only after following the most cumbersome procedures.[5]

The principal obstacle to the Progressives of 1924 was the use of legal machinery in California, Louisiana, and Ohio. California made no provision for placing electors on the ballot by petition An appeal to the state supreme court to allow a petition was un-

4. Kenneth C. MacKay, *The Progressive Movement of 1924* (Octagon, 1966), pp. 179–83.
5. Nevada required signatures from 10 percent of the number of voters in the previous presidential contest. Florida specified that a petition be filed in each of its 54 counties, each containing signatures of at least 25 voters.

successful and the party was finally forced to appear under the Socialist column. In Louisiana the secretary of state ruled that only independents with no party affiliation could validly sign Progressive petitions; the La Follette-Wheeler organization had amassed petitions signed largely by registered Democrats. In Ohio, by contrast, the Progressives were not denied a ballot position but assurance of an honest vote; neither state officials nor the state supreme court would allow them to have poll watchers at election booths.

In the end the La Follette forces succeeded in getting their candidate on the ballot in all states. Nevertheless, a combination of public officials' action and legal technicalities served to prevent the creation of a single party label that could readily be identified across the nation. Thus La Follette votes were cast for a variety of party names—Progressives, Independents, Independent-Progressives, and Socialists.

By the mid-1920s ballot laws and related aspects of the electoral process were weighted in favor of preserving the existing major parties. The rights of minorities were not completely denied; no state explicitly prohibited third parties. But the task of gaining entry to the election arena was far more difficult than necessary.

The tenor of the controversy changed in the late 1930s and 1940s. The tensions of war and a general fear of "isms" extended to the conduct of elections. Legislatures prohibited "un-American" parties—those connected with foreign powers, advocating the violent overthrow of the government, or considered subversive in any way.

Before 1940 a small number of states excluded parties that "advocate the overthrow of the government by force or violence." In 1940 three states barred the Communist party from the ballot in spite of the party's disavowal of the use of violence as early as 1938 and its unqualified support of "the right of the majority to direct the destinies of our country."[6] The purging of the party spread rapidly. The new laws were challenged in the courts, and in a

---

6. Hugh H. Bone, "Small Political Parties Casualties of War," *National Municipal Review*, vol. 32 (November 1943), p. 526.

number of states were overruled.[7] Nevertheless, the reduction was dramatic in Communist, Socialist, and other leftist party candidacies and in the votes received by third parties.[8] The Prohibitionists were the only minor party that did not experience a rapid decline in strength.

The difficulty new contenders faced in entering elections became apparent in the presidential election in 1948. Legislation introduced in the U.S. Congress was designed to exclude Henry Wallace and the Progressive party. The attorney general at hearings interpreted the bill's prohibition of any party that had not repudiated support from the Communists to apply to the Progressives. The bill, however, was never reported out of committee.

With that threat aside, the Wallace campaign faced the traditional hurdles to third parties in the ballot laws.[9] Filing deadlines had become a major obstacle. The earliest required filing date, in California, was in March, eight months prior to the election. Fourteen states required filing by the first of July, forcing a new party to organize long before the major parties had selected their candidates. Formation of a new party after the major conventions —like the Roosevelt Progressive split in the Republican ranks in 1912—was unlikely.

Some of the more difficult situations confronted by the Wallace forces were reminiscent of the La Follette experience of 1924. California with its early filing required petition signatures equivalent to 10 percent of the votes cast in the 1946 gubernatorial election. West Virginia, in a law clearly aimed at third parties, declared that signing a new party petition was tantamount to membership in the party; Wallace petition signers could not participate in the Democratic primary, in which crucial state and local contests were decided. A different obstacle arose when a suit was filed

---

7. Laws were overruled in Illinois (*Feinglass* v. *Reinecke*, 48 F. Supp. 438 [D.C. Ill. 1943]); California (*Communist Party* v. *Peck*, 20 Cal. 2d 536, 127 P.2d 889 [1942]); and Washington (*State ex rel Huff* v. *Reeves*, 106 Pac. 2d 729 [1940]); see *Yale Law Journal*, vol. 57 (June 1948).

8. Bone, "Small Political Parties," p. 524.

9. Karl M. Schmidt, *Henry Wallace: Quixotic Crusade 1948* (Syracuse University Press, 1960), p. 131.

challenging the Oklahoma secretary of state for accepting the Wallace petition because of Wallace's alleged Communist affiliations. The state election board refused Wallace a ballot position because the secretary of state had not approved the party's non-Communist affidavit prior to the filing deadline as required by state law. The state supreme court upheld this ruling and Wallace did not appear on the Oklahoma ballot.

Illinois also thwarted the Wallace effort. The Progressive party amassed some 75,000 petition signatures—far in excess of the state's 25,000 signature requirement, with at least 200 from each of 50 counties. The State Electoral Board, however, disqualified the party, first ruling that persons who had voted in the primary of either major party could not sign the petition, and then finding the petition lacked the valid number of signatures in certain counties. The party challenged this decision in court on the grounds of equal protection under the Fourteenth Amendment and discrimination against the voters of Cook County and the remaining forty-eight most populous counties, but to no avail. First, a special three-member federal district court refused to reinstate the party on the ballot. On appeal, the Supreme Court upheld the lower court's ruling, with Chief Justice Fred M. Vinson declaring on behalf of the majority of the Court that no precise or literal interpretation of constitutional protections was necessary in this instance.

In Ohio the party met a series of obstacles. First the secretary of state refused the party a ballot position. The party appealed to the state supreme court and won a reversal of the secretary's ruling. Next confronting a petition requirement of 500,000 signatures, the Progressives decided to enter Wallace as an independent. This time the secretary of state ruled that the election code did not provide for an independent candidacy. Again the court overruled the secretary, but it concluded that the candidate's name could not appear on the ballot. Thus Progressive voters had to identify and vote for twenty-five electors with no party or candidate designation to guide them. It was possible, however, to vote a straight Democratic or Republican ticket.

In contrast to the frustrating experience of the Wallace Progressives in 1948, the States' Rights party campaign of that year suggests that third parties can readily get on the ballot when the incumbent lawmakers are friendly. Many southern legislatures welcomed the States' Rights party, whose candidate Strom Thurmond began his campaign after southern Democrats had walked out of the national convention.

Placing the States' Rights ticket on the ballot in the South could have been extremely difficult. In Florida, for instance, the Progressives had failed to persuade the required 5 percent of the registered voters to change their affiliation prior to the state's May primary. Following the Democratic national convention, however, the Florida legislature amended the statutes, allowing nominees simply to file without formality. The States' Rights party thus easily found a place on the ballot, as did the Progressives.

Georgia also revised its statutes for the benefit of the States' Rights party, permitting simple certification of the names of presidential electors for a ballot position. The Progressives meantime had been attempting to fulfill an exceedingly difficult requirement of verifying that all those signing its petitions were registered voters. Again, the benefits extended to the Progressives, though not to the party's slate for state offices.

The experience in the South in 1948 is a dramatic illustration of the extent to which the dominant major parties can manipulate the authority of the state to serve their own ends.

Few of the statutes affecting third parties were altered between 1948 and 1968. Thirty-seven states continued to allow petitions. Filing deadlines remained a major obstacle; California and at least fifteen other states required filing before either July 1 or the state primary. (A few states such as Hawaii, New York, and New Hampshire allowed filing up to the closing four or five weeks of the fall campaign.) The number of signatures required remained high in many states, including Ohio and California. (One major reversal, in South Dakota, reduced a 20 percent petition requirement in 1948 to 10 percent in 1968.) Finally, 60 percent of the states retained legislation barring Communist or subversive parties.[10] As a result, in 1968 voters of only twenty-five states could choose among the nine minor parties other than the AIP contesting the election.[11]

The AIP in its effort to place George Wallace on the ballot clearly felt the impact of these statutes. Wallace spent the last months of 1967 persuading 107,000 Californians to reregister under the AIP banner.[12] This accomplishment was a dramatic kickoff for his national campaign, but the drive faced numerous other difficulties. The party was not granted a ballot position in all the states until the final weeks of the campaign, and even then, only by the grace of a favorable ruling from the Supreme Court. In all, across the nation, Wallace collected close to 3 million signatures—a number approximately equal to 4 percent of the votes cast in the 1968 presidential election—in order to gain access to the ballot. Such a feat was not demanded of either major party or matched by any other third party. And differing state laws combined to deny a singular label to the new, yet clearly nationwide party. This necessitated that Wallace's ticket appear under a variety of labels—the American Independent party, the American party, the Conservative party, the Courage party, the Georgia Wallace party, and the George C. Wallace party.

That Wallace, a candidate preferred by up to 20 percent of the public according to preelection polls, accomplished the feat only after heavy expenditure of scarce time and resources attests to the continuing obstacles in gaining access to the ballot. Yet the Supreme Court's unprecedented ruling in 1968 that the AIP be placed on the ballot in Ohio has altered the direction of ballot laws. The electoral system should now move in the direction of

10. John P. Mackenzie, "Reds Are Ruled Eligible For Minnesota Ballot," *Washington Post*, Sept. 25, 1968. However, the Justice Department advised the state of Minnesota that it could not bar the Communist party on the basis of the 1954 Communist Control Act, implying that the law was not likely to be sustained under a court test.

11. Willard H. Mobley, "Minor Parties Running Candidates from Trotzkyites to Pat Paulsen," *Washington Post*, Nov. 5, 1968.

12. Lewis Chester, Godfrey Hodgson, and Bruce Page, *An American Melodrama* (Dell, 1969), p. 317.

the original public mandate—open and honest elections that do not place undue burdens on new and third parties. Lawmakers will most likely be placed under increasing pressure to develop regulations that promote honesty and efficiency and do minimal damage to the civil liberties of small parties and the voting public.

## NEW ROLE OF THE COURTS

The important development in the 1968 election was the Supreme Court's aggressive stand against election laws that do little more than impede new and third parties. Chief Justice Earl Warren framed the question in *Williams* v. *Rhodes*: "To what extent may a State consistent with equal protection and the First Amendment guarantee of freedom of association, impose restrictions upon a candidate's desire to be placed upon the ballot?"[13] The Court did not stipulate what the actual balance should be. Rather, it found that the Ohio statutes, taken together, clearly served to exclude all but the two major parties.

The Court rejected Ohio's objective of "maintaining a two-party system in order to promote compromise and political stability"[14] on the grounds that only the Republican and Democratic parties were being maintained, not two-partyism as such. Though the Court found Ohio's goal of majority victory laudable, it was not worthy enough to "justify laws that virtually stifled the growth of new parties."[15] Ohio had also claimed that an extensive party organization and a primary nomination were necessary to ensure membership participation in party decisions. The Court held that, in practice, those requisites served only to deter new parties. Finally, the state's claim that without restrictive laws an unmanageable number of candidates might qualify, only to present the electorate with a confusing choice, was refuted with numerous illustrations of minimum requirements that had not resulted in a mushrooming number of candidates or confusion among the electorate.

13. *Williams* v. *Rhodes, Governor Ohio,* 393 U.S. 23 (1968), quoted in Malcolm B. Wiseheart, Jr., "Constitutional Law: Third Political Parties as Second Class Citizens," *University of Florida Law Review,* vol. 21 (Spring–Summer 1969), p. 703.
14. Ibid., p. 705.
15. Ibid.

Reversing its earlier doctrine, the Court required "that a state must show a compelling interest when it excludes persons from the franchise." The Court ordered that the American Independent party be placed on the ballot along with its presidential and vice presidential candidates, and authorized write-in voting for the Socialists.[16] (The Socialists were not given a ballot position because they had filed their action with the Court too late for such a change to be feasible.)

Though the ruling in this case was undoubtedly an advance for civil liberties, the limits of the First and Fourteenth Amendment application remain uncertain. A case involving the ballot laws of Georgia—*Jenness* v. *Fortson*—provides some excellent clues. Justice Potter Stewart, delivering the Court's opinion, contrasted Georgia's laws with Ohio's:

Unlike Ohio, Georgia freely provides for write-in votes. Unlike Ohio, Georgia does not require every candidate to be the nominee of a political party, but fully recognizes independent candidacies. Unlike Ohio, Georgia does not fix an unreasonably early filing deadline for candidates not endorsed by established parties. Unlike Ohio, Georgia does not impose upon a small party or a new party the Procrustean requirement of establishing elaborate primary election machinery. Finally, and in sum, Georgia's election laws, unlike Ohio's, do not operate to freeze the political status quo.[17]

In sum, Georgia law was not seen as serving to unduly restrict access to the ballot. While the qualification requirements for new and established parties differed, the requirements for a "political body" appeared to the Court no more stringent than those for a "political party." In general, the Court found, the law operated to ensure an efficient and honest election—the primary interest of the state—while maintaining a minimal infringement of individual liberties. The balance between the obligations of the state and the rights of the individual under Georgia law satisfied the Court.

Of the greatest importance in the area of ballot laws is the doc-

16. Elizabeth Yadlosky, *The Qualification of Minor and New Political Parties and Independent Candidates for a Place on the General Election Ballot*, ed. Robert Thornton and Stuart Glass (Library of Congress, Legislative Reference Service, 1970), p. vii.

17. *Jenness* v. *Fortson*, 403 U.S. 431, 438 (1971).

trine of "compelling interest." The burden of proof lies on the state, which must justify its compelling interest in denying access to the ballot. Litigation under this new doctrine could lead to court challenges to most state requirements for access. While it is hard to imagine that minimal requirements such as petitions containing 1 percent of the registered voters will be overthrown, those requiring as much as 10 percent may well be. Courts may also rule against laws requiring re-registration in order simply to sign the petition of a new party.

In a variety of other ways the ballot laws have been challenged. For example, the Illinois law governing petition signatures that was effectively used against Henry A. Wallace was held unconstitutional in 1969.[18] Following the one-man-one-vote doctrine,[19] the Court held that the state cannot devise petition schemes that require signatures by geographic units (counties), which in effect give less weight to the signatures of persons in the more populated urban areas.

The activism of the Supreme Court has tipped the scale in favor of the First and Fourteenth Amendment rights of new political bodies to compete and, in turn, of voters to have a wider selection of candidates among whom to choose. The government's role in elections appears to be swinging back to one of assuring honesty and efficiency, leaving the number of parties dependent on other forces.

The shift is not nearly so evident in practice as in principle. Ohio in 1972 reduced its requirements for signatures on a nominating petition from 15 percent of those voting in the previous gubernatorial contest to 7 percent and moved the date for filing from 120 to 90 days prior to the primary. New York, like Ohio challenged on a number of its regulations, changed its requirement for petition signatures from 12,000 with at least 50 from each county to 20,000 with at least 100 in half of the congressional districts. Thus, a new party no longer needed to organize in every county, but it needed the support of a greater total number of

18. *Moore* v. *Ogilvie*, 394 U.S. 814 (1969).
19. *Baker* v. *Carr*, 369 U.S. 186 (1962); and *Reynolds* v. *Sims*, 377 U.S. 533 (1964).

voters. Meanwhile, Alaska has moved in the opposite direction, stiffening the requirements for ballot position.

## A NATIONAL BALLOT CODE

Excessive requirements placed before third parties are now clearly unconstitutional, yet a myriad of state restrictions remains. The courts, in eliminating the most inequitable practices denying or impeding access to the ballot, have avoided explicit guidelines, leaving much room for variation. The Supreme Court felt that a 5 percent petition requirement was acceptable in Georgia in light of the state's code. Under other circumstances a 5 percent requirement might be considered an undue restriction on third parties. The case-by-case approach is a sound way of accommodating the nuances in ballot access laws, and of avoiding judicial encroachment on legislative matters.

Nevertheless, certain minimum guarantees of an open and equitable electoral system must be established. For instance, laws that allow the major parties to enter their nominees after their national conventions but require other candidates to enter earlier clearly place third parties at a disadvantage. Petition laws that require small parties to accumulate signatures in the amount of 10–15 percent of the electorate in some states are also inequitable. There is little justification for requiring petitions of more than 1–2 percent under any circumstance, and disparities between states seem especially onerous when the party is seeking to enter the national presidential contest. These requirements are not meant to serve as pernicious barriers to newcomers, but as an expedient method by which a party can demonstrate a minimal level of public support.

Subjective tests of a party nominee's loyalty, like those aimed at Communist sympathizers or at activities considered un-American, are also contrary to democratic practices. They undermine the basic tenet of voter sovereignty and in turn the legitimacy of the political system. Any prior restraint of parties or candidates because of their policy positions or ideology can only be construed as undemocratic censorship.

The only effective means of redressing these many wrongs is

through a national election code. Its underlying premises must be fairness and openness, without regard for party size—beyond a minimal expression of voter interest—or political orientation. The voters can then decide who is worthy of public office.

## Access to the Broadcasting Media

A still more ominous threat to third parties is the loss of access to the broadcasting media. It has become the most important means of gaining a public forum.

In the earliest American election campaigns, candidates stumped the countryside. Anyone who could corner an audience could spread his views. With the emergence of mass circulation newspapers in the nineteenth century and with a rapidly expanding population to reach, political groups began circulating their views via newspaper, pamphlet, and book. The printed word supplemented the spoken, but the essential openness of the marketplace of ideas survived. The only constraint on political dialogue was the energy and resources of individuals. More important, participants in the dialogue needed only a printing press. Government was not called upon to regulate the marketplace of public debate.

New technology, the continued growth of the population, and government regulation radically altered this situation. The broadcast industry—first radio, then network television—has created an entirely new method of communication and form of political debate. This new forum is not readily available to all citizens and political groups. That access to the media would be limited, because of the relatively few frequencies available in the electromagnetic spectrum, was early recognized. Concern over who would have access grew immediately. Congress attempted to resolve the issue, particularly for political broadcasting, in Section 315(a) of the Communications Act of 1934:

If any licensee shall permit any person who is a legally qualified candidate for any public office to use a broadcasting station, he shall afford equal opportunities to all other such candidates for that office in the use of such broadcasting station: *Provided,* That such licensee shall have no power of censorship over the material broadcast under the provisions of this section. No obligation is hereby imposed upon any licensee to allow the use of its station by any such candidate.

The mandate is explicit: all bona fide contenders for any political contest are to be guaranteed equal access to the media. The new technology would obviously limit freedom of expression—not everyone would have access—but the flow of ideas and debate over public programs and between contending political groups would be assured.

Although equal access does not guarantee equal exposure, at least some time seems to have been intended for all contenders. Congress recognized in the Communications Act that the right to be heard is as much a part of the representative process as the right to be on the ballot. Thus Congress created the Federal Communications Commission (FCC) "to insure that licensees serve the public interest, convenience and necessity." In the political dialogue, the industry was "to afford reasonable opportunity to the discussion of conflicting views." In the three and a half decades since the inception of the Communications Act both the use of radio and television and the interpretation of government's role in regulating political broadcasting have changed substantially.

In 1934 radio was a reality, television a dream. By 1968, television had rocketed to the position of the single most important means of political communication. Ninety-five percent of American homes had television sets (up from 87 percent in 1960, 9 percent in 1950).[20] Television was the major source of news about national candidates for 65 percent of those in a Roper survey (newspapers for 24 percent, radio for 4 percent, and magazines for 5 percent). And 57 percent of those polled considered television the communication source providing the "clearest understanding of national issues and candidates."[21]

Meanwhile the cost of conducting a political campaign has grown tremendously, and the largest portion of the increase is attributable to television broadcasting. As the total direct expendi-

20. *Nielsen TV 1969* (Chicago: A. C. Nielsen Co., 1969), p. 10.
21. Burns W. Roper, *A Ten-Year View of Public Attitudes Towards Television and Other Mass Media 1959–1968* (New York: Television Information Office, 1969), pp. 8–10.

tures by presidential contenders more than tripled between 1956 and 1968, from $14 million to $48 million, the cost in television and radio programming rose from $5 million to over $20 million.[22] Rapidly changing, complex issues and enormous political stakes have encouraged politicians to use the television screen as their primary medium of communication. How else to reach a population of over 200 million? Media exposure is no guarantee of victory, but its absence surely spells doom in national or even statewide contests.

How have third parties fared in this new era? Have viewpoints that are not reflected in the major political parties been aired in public dialogue via broadcasting? In terms of actual viewing time the answer is equivocal. But government interest is waning in guaranteeing an equal or even proportionate share of broadcasting time for third parties.

Third-party contenders for the presidency and vice presidency fared well on television and radio time in 1956 and 1968, but poorly in 1960 and 1964. They received a little more than one-third of the total "free time" and "commercially sponsored free time" on television in 1956 and a little more than one-fourth in 1968. In 1960 their share of this time was only one-fourteenth and in 1964 roughly one-thirteenth.[23] The same proportions hold for the time on radio provided the presidential candidates, except in 1960 when third parties received less than 4 percent of the total time awarded. In terms of free time, third parties fared well in two of the four presidential elections between 1956 and 1968.

Even where aggregate data indicate compliance with the spirit of the Communications Act, experience of third-party contenders sometimes reveals a different pattern. The Socialist Labor party received radio and television time in the 1956 campaign, but complained:

The time was not equal in all respects, but it was at least equal in amount. And we did not secure it in all instances without putting up

22. Delmer D. Dunn, *Financing Presidential Campaigns* (Brookings Institution, 1972), table 1, p. 31.
23. Ibid., fig. 10, p. 103.

a battle for it. Nevertheless, with the aid of section 315(a) we finally secured the time. Following the appearances of our candidates on these networks, we tracked down at least 77 radio stations and 79 television stations affiliated with the various networks that had broadcast or telecast the acceptance speeches of the major party candidates by direct pickup from the network release, or by making tape or other recording for later release, but failed in either respect with the network release of the Socialist Labor Party candidates' acceptance talks.

After considerable correspondence and effort most of these 156 stations did release the Socialist Labor Party programs but we had to supply kinescopes and/or tapes of the programs at our own expense, or run the risk of running out of time by continued correspondence and "negotiation." And for all we know, there may have been as many more stations that failed to fulfill their clear statutory obligation in 1956, but it was simply beyond our physical and financial means to follow them all up.[24]

Making third-party contenders responsible for enforcing a law designed to uphold basic democratic rights clearly works against any intention of guaranteeing equal access and equal treatment to all political viewpoints.

### MEDIA ACCESS FOR THE MAJOR PARTIES

From the major-party contenders' point of view, the alarming factor in political broadcasting is the soaring cost of television time. Growing media costs have meant a growing influence on major-party candidates of a relatively small number of wealthy contributors. Public awareness and condemnation of the practice has sent lawmakers in search of some method of providing candidates for office—in particular, candidates for the presidency—with free media time.

The broadcasting companies have fairly consistently argued that they cannot absorb the costs of providing free media time to all the candidates that get on the presidential ballot; they oppose government regulations that would restrict their control over programming; and they oppose any obligation to provide equal time, as opposed to equal access, to all presidential candidates. Their solu-

24. *Equal Time*, Hearings before the Subcommittee on Communications of the Senate Committee on Commerce, 88 Cong. 1 sess. (1963), pp. 149–50.

tion to the problem is repeal of Section 315(a) of the Communications Act. Repeatedly they have expressed their desire to provide free time to the major candidates,[25] and they promise to do so in exchange for repeal of 315(a).

In 1959 Congress, conceding to the broadcasters, amended the equal time statute. Candidate time on newscasts, news interviews, or news documentaries is now excluded—provided the candidate's appearance is "incidental to the presentation of the subject covered" in the program.[26] Thus, the broadcast time that is being provided to candidates under this exemption is no longer provided as the broadcasting licensee's obligation to the public. It is awarded at the discretion of the licensee. The right of all political contenders to be heard in a democratic society has moved closer to a privilege conferred at the discretion of a select group of executives who happen to hold franchises on the public airwaves. Just as the promise of additional coverage for major parties was realized when news broadcasts were exempted from equal time requirements in 1959, the potentials of free political broadcast time, and thus drastically reduced campaign costs, loom even greater for the major parties with the complete abolition of 315(a).

The networks have a persuasive example from the temporary suspension of Section 315(a) in 1960 that removal of 315(a) would assure the "important" candidates more television time at a reduced cost. Controversies over types of coverage allocated to candidates and requirements for qualification would go to the FCC for settlement. They would be resolved under the commission's "fairness doctrine," a subjective test that has left many decisions to the discretion of the broadcast industry.[27] Candidates, who rely on broadcasting as their foremost means of campaigning, are being asked to trade away their own and all future candidates' rights to

25. Dunn, *Financing Presidential Campaigns*, pp. 82–84.

26. *Freedom of Communications*, Final Report of the Committee on Commerce, 87 Cong. 1 sess. (1961), pt. 5, p. 225.

27. The fairness doctrine is the primary FCC guideline for matters not covered by the Communications Act. It is not part of statutory law, however, and the guidelines are those that broadcasters deem proper and the public tolerates. See *Fairness Doctrine*, staff report prepared for the Subcommittee on Communications of the Senate Committee on Commerce, 90 Cong. 2 sess. (1968).

equal access for a promise of good faith on the part of broadcasters. Wealthy financiers would play a less important role under this system, but control by the broadcasters is at least as undesirable.

Dozens of bills introduced in Congress over the past fifteen years have included provisions for elimination of 315(a). The objective was partly met in 1959, and will almost certainly be fully met in the near future. In 1970 one such bill cleared both houses of Congress only to be vetoed by the President. In 1971 the Senate version of a similar measure (the Federal Election Campaign Act of 1971) again included the repeal of equal time for presidential contests; the clause was eventually stricken in the Senate-House conference but only under pressure from the White House.[28]

In these cases, 315(a) was retained not so much in fear of the adverse effects its removal might have on third parties as in response to the warning of White House aides that any removal of the equal-time guarantee must extend to all federal elective contests— otherwise the entire bill faced a presidential veto. Apparently President Nixon did not see repeal of equal time to his advantage in the 1972 campaign and did not want to be confronted with a debate challenge from his Democratic rival, an eventuality that was likely to occur with abolition of 315(a), as it had in the 1960 election when 315(a) was temporarily suspended. To avoid this threat, he placed all congressmen in a similar position, a strategy that obviously worked. Nonetheless, the pressures of spiraling media costs time and again lead Congress back to the logic of the broadcasters.

As lawmakers search for remedies, the 1960 experience is likely to seem increasingly pertinent. The free time available to the major parties grew more nearly equal in 1960. Third-party candidates, of course, received only one-fourteenth of the free time, compared to one-third in the previous election. Public interest fastens, however, on the fact that the major parties will be treated equitably in relation to one another without 315(a) guarantees. The U.S. Court of Appeals, following the fairness doctrine, has affirmed that disposition; it ruled the Democratic party's claim to answer President

28. Don Oberdorfer, "Chronicle of Compromise," *Washington Post*, Dec. 16, 1971.

Nixon's televised addresses to the nation on the Indochina war was legitimate.[29] A similar request by Congressman Paul McCloskey who challenged Nixon in the 1972 Republican primaries was rejected.

Under the elusive notion of fairness, who might be considered to have a legitimate claim to respond to the President? Did George Wallace as titular head of the AIP after the 1968 election qualify, or Eugene McCarthy as a quasi-independent presidential contender, or Linda Jenness, 1972 candidate of the Socialist Workers party? Probably the answer of the FCC and the courts in all three cases would be negative.

### EXPANDING THE PUBLIC DIALOGUE

Bills to eliminate 315(a) are widely supported despite the declared commitment of many legislators to expand political participation and maintain an open political dialogue.[30] An alternative campaign reform bill is needed that would assure a minimum level of exposure for every legally recognized contender. It must also provide access to the media for those other than the rich or their spokesmen.

*Voters' Time.* A proposal devised in 1969 would provide contenders for the presidency with a reasonable amount of television time, commensurate with their demonstrated or potential strength, without charge to the candidates.[31] This "Voters' Time" plan assumes the public has a right to hear the leading sides in public con-

29. The court ruled on November 15, 1971, that the time granted Democratic National Chairman Lawrence O'Brien by the American Broadcasting Companies for his "loyal opposition" response in July 1970 to televised speeches made by President Nixon was justified. They ruled against a Republican petition to reply to O'Brien, however, arguing that this would in effect provide double coverage for the Republicans. Warren Weaver, Jr., *New York Times,* Nov. 16, 1971.

30. See, for example, testimony of Representative John B. Anderson of Illinois in *Political Broadcasting—1971,* Hearings before the Subcommittee on Communications and Power of the House Committee on Interstate and Foreign Commerce, 92 Cong. 1 sess. (1971), p. 86.

31. Twentieth Century Fund, *Voters' Time: Report of the Twentieth Century Fund Commission on Campaign Costs in the Electronic Era* (Twentieth Century Fund, 1969), p. 22.

troversies and political contests. It classifies all contenders by their degree of public support, and assigns them time accordingly.

One category includes the two top vote-getters (almost invariably the Democratic and Republican candidates), a second the sizable vote-getters (receiving one-eighth of the votes cast), and a third those with a good potential. The requirement common to all three categories is qualification for the ballot in at least three-fourths of the states whose collective votes would total a majority of the electoral college. The party is thereby required to have at least a mathematical chance of victory in the presidential race, a requirement that shuts out the many candidates in each election who enroll in only a few states—twelve candidates enrolled in only a few states in 1960, eight in 1964, and nine in 1968. These guidelines would have put the Socialist party of Eugene Debs and Norman Thomas in the third category seven times, but never in the second.[32] The Roosevelt Progressives in 1912, the La Follette Progressives in 1924, the Henry Wallace Progressives in 1948, and George Wallace's AIP in 1968 would also have fallen in the third category, and all of these except the Wallace Progressives could have fallen in the second category in a following election. Only the Democrats and Republicans would have qualified for the first category in this century. The criteria for entry would have excluded the Prohibitionists, American Vegetarians, and all the other fringe parties that regularly enter presidential elections.

Network time would be awarded to the parties according to the categories within which they fell—six half-hour prime-time slots, distributed through the last thirty-five days of the campaign, in the first category, two half-hour slots in the second, and one in the third. The government would assume the cost of these broadcasts, to be billed at one-half the prevailing commercial rate. The campaign period would be reduced appreciably, and air time allotted so that no candidate could squeeze all his time into the closing days of the election.

The Voters' Time proposal is a step in the direction of balancing the rights of contenders to be heard and of the public to know

32. Ibid., p. 23.

within limits that reflect the public support of parties. As that support fluctuates so too would the free time allocated. The formula is neither so free that it provides equal time under the law to every contender nor so harsh that it awards time only to the major contenders. Balancing the multiplicity of interests that need to be considered, it provides publicly sponsored television and radio time for all serious contenders, helping the voter form an opinion of both candidates and issues.

*Publicly Sponsored Equal Time.* The major shortcoming of the Voter's Time proposal is its willingness to forgo the equal protection rights of the First and Fourteenth amendments. Apparently the repeal of Section 315(a), with its long-standing guarantee of access but small rewards for third parties, seems a reasonable trade-off for a concrete promise of a specified amount of time rationed according to party strength. The benefits, however, may be short lived. Once the precedent is established that legally recognized contenders are not to be treated equally under the law, but according to categories of popular support, lawmakers may feel free to change the ratios. Time might be reallocated in such a way as to deny adequate coverage to new and third parties. Also, the unequal allocation of government funds required under the plan may be judged unconstitutional.[33]

No differentiation should be allowed among legally recognized candidates for the presidency. Section 315(a) should be amended, in accord with the Voters' Time proposal, to apply to those candidates on the ballot in three-fourths of the states that have a mathematical chance of winning in the electoral college. The pool of persons eligible for television and radio time would correspond to those who in fact are the only validly eligible candidates for the presidency. All candidates qualifying would then be provided an equal amount of publicly sponsored time—for instance, four half-hour periods apportioned over the month preceding an election. Only in this way will the guarantees of the First and Fourteenth amendments be assured.

33. See Albert J. Rosenthal, *Federal Regulation of Campaign Finance: Some Constitutional Questions* (Princeton, N.J.: Citizens' Research Foundation, 1972).

The plan would also accommodate nationally televised debates between candidates. Under existing law the networks cannot provide free time for debates between the two major candidates without providing a similar opportunity for all contenders. The broadcast industry, alleging that the cost is prohibitive, provides no debate time. It only did so in 1960 because Section 315(a) was temporarily suspended by Congress. Under the equal time plan, two or more candidates could agree to pool their publicly sponsored time to hold a national debate. This would not create a case of unequal access, but would simply represent the candidates' choice of how best to use their television time. Thus two candidates, such as the major-party nominees, could choose to debate one another while declining to debate third-party contenders.

Just as lawmakers are now required to show compelling cause for abridging access to the ballot, so should they be required to show compelling reason for impeding dialogue between legally recognized national presidential candidates. Both the need for new ideas and public programs and the right of the public to be informed would be well served by such a policy. Nor would these objectives be forsaken in the equally important drive to reduce campaign costs.

## The Electoral College Debate

Much of the recent controversy over presidential elections has centered on the consequences that changing the electoral college system might have for third parties. The proposals for dealing with the electoral college problem run the gamut from preservation of the status quo to conversion to a direct vote plan.[34]

34. See Lawrence D. Longley and Alan G. Braun, *The Politics of Electoral College Reform* (Yale University Press, 1972); Neal R. Pierce, *The People's President: The Electoral College in American History and the Direct Vote Alternative* (Simon and Schuster, 1968); Wallace S. Sayre and Judith H. Parris, *Voting for President: The Electoral College and the American Political System* (Brookings Institution, 1970); and Max S. Power, "Logic and Legitimacy: On Understanding the Electoral College Controversy," in Donald R. Matthews, ed., *Perspectives on Presidential Selection* (Brookings Institution, 1973).

The direct vote method of selecting a President is aimed at making the election as democratic, and as uncomplicated, as possible. The basic goals are to ensure that the one-man-one-vote rule is followed, that the most preferred candidate wins, and that no possibility exists for manipulating the outcome according to the whims of a select group (the electors). To eradicate the shortcomings in the present system, the direct vote proposal, as introduced in the Ninety-first Congress, would provide for election by direct popular vote, with a plurality deciding the winner.[35] It would remove the threat of "faithless" electors; the unit rules that in many states bind the state's electoral votes; the automatic award of two electoral votes to each state; the casting of a single vote for a state's House delegation in contingent elections; and the possibility that the popular vote winner will lose.[36]

Preservation of the status quo is more a practical, political matter than an appeal to democratic principle. Major changes in the electoral college system "may induce subtle shifts in the electoral strategies, rendering prediction based on past experience hazardous."[37] The party system is apt to change dramatically under a direct-vote plan because "populous states and their major metropolitan areas would be less powerful in presidential elections and perhaps in presidential policymaking than they are under the existing system."[38]

The effect of a direct popular vote on third parties is a key point of debate. The electoral college is defended as a guardian of the two-party system, which is considered eminently desirable. Not only would the direct vote eliminate the winner-take-all feature of the statewide electoral contest and the systematic overrepresentation of large parties; it would also in all likelihood lead to many more third-party candidates.

35. The House of Representatives approved a constitutional amendment for direct election of the President by an overwhelming 339 to 70 in September of 1969. The Senate version of the amendment—which was cosponsored by 43 members of the Senate—never emerged from committee because of a filibuster.
36. Longley and Braun, *Politics of Electoral College Reform*, p. 66.
37. Alexander M. Bickel, *Reform and Continuity: The Electoral College, the Convention, and the Party System* (Harper and Row, 1971), p. 35.
38. Sayre and Parris, *Voting for President*, p. 145.

The run-off would be typical; the major party nomination would count for much less than it now does; there would be little inducement to unity in each party following the conventions; coalitions would be formed not at conventions but during the period between the general election and the run-off; and the dominant positions of the two major parties would not long be sustained.[39]

Changes following the implementation of a direct vote plan may not be so drastic.[40] Under both the electoral college plan and the direct vote plan, third parties can raise issues, arouse interest among previously uninvolved persons, and deprive one of the major parties of a plurality victory (in state electoral votes and in direct votes nationally). The third party's potential for directly affecting the outcome of an election at present lies in its ability to act as a "power broker" in the electoral college, providing the winning electoral votes if neither of the major parties has a majority. The third party need only win popular vote pluralities, and thus electoral votes, in a limited number of states. These votes then become the bargaining chips for negotiations with both major parties in close contests. Should such a situation arise, the third party could conceivably wield great power.

The electoral college system allows a third party's electoral vote to far exceed its actual popular support. For instance, by focusing its efforts in a few southern states the States' Rights party of Strom Thurmond was able to turn a popular vote of 2.4 percent into almost three times that amount—7.0 percent of the votes in the electoral college.[41] By contrast, the 2.4 percent of the popular votes the Wallace Progressives received in the same election were distributed in such a fashion that the party won no state pluralities and thus no electoral vote. In short, the third party that wishes to play a strategic role in determining the outcome of a presidential contest has an incentive to concentrate its campaign in a limited number

---

39. Alexander M. Bickel, "Wait a Minute," *New Republic*, May 10, 1969, p. 13.

40. A direct vote plan sponsored by Senator Birch Bayh (Democrat of Indiana) is described in *Direct Popular Election of the President*, S. Rept. 91-1123, 91 Cong. 2 sess. (1970).

41. The States' Rights electoral slates won in Alabama, Louisiana, Mississippi, and South Carolina and received one electoral vote from Tennessee.

of states in hopes of controlling a block of electoral votes. Not only might a relatively small but geographically concentrated third party play a strategic role; the third party's strength also may be extremely exaggerated in certain situations.

The popular votes of third parties are seldom distributed, however, so that the parties receive a disproportionate electoral vote. Though they have attempted to do so, third parties have never been able to form a coalition with one of the major parties in the electoral college. But the possibility of a coalition was clearly demonstrated in 1968.

The direct vote plan, in eliminating the electoral college, allows for neither an exaggeration of a third party's strength nor a power-broker role for the party. It does provide an incentive for a third party to amass enough votes to force a runoff election. The party has little incentive to restrict its efforts to a small number of states. Such parties are likely to be even less instrumental in affecting the outcome of elections under a direct vote plan than under the electoral college. The plurality rule proposed for presidential selection stipulates that a runoff election will be held only if no candidate receives 40 percent or more of the popular vote; it is a compromise between the goals of providing a strong presidential mandate and of avoiding runoff elections. To prevent a major-party victory, then, at least 20 percent of the popular vote would have to go to third parties, while at the same time neither of the major parties received 40 percent or more. Thus, to force a runoff in 1968, George Wallace would have had to better his 9.9 million votes by 50 percent, or close to 5 million votes. Such a formidable task suggests that a direct vote system, if anything, would reduce the strategic importance of third parties. No longer could a regional candidate hope to gain disproportionate influence, nor would a third party be likely to force a runoff.

If a runoff were necessitated, the interval between the first and contingent elections would no doubt be a time of maneuvering and coalition building. But the same is true if no party received a majority of electoral votes. The crucial difference is in the instrument of ultimate selection: under the electoral college, a coalition of electors, with the inevitable implication of shady deals and corrupt politics, and under the direct vote plan, the entire electorate.

Third parties appear to have the best chance of directly influencing the selection of the President under the electoral college, not the direct vote system. More important in the systems' effect on third parties is the nature of the presidential contest. Third parties gain their strength through issues rather than in actual office-seeking. Selection of the President by the direct vote plan is not likely to alter this situation. When intense minorities go unrepresented, third parties can be expected to arise, in spite of their slight prospects for actually holding the balance of power. Although the direct vote plan would bring the electoral process more in line with contemporary notions of democratic procedure, it should be neither lauded nor condemned for providing added incentives for third-party participation.

☆

*Chapter Five*

☆

# A MODIFIED
# TWO-PARTY SYSTEM

THE EUROPEAN multiparty system is not the only alternative to the two-party system with episodic third-party activity. New York State has a highly competitive party system with two major contenders and third-party contestants that are able to sustain themselves over time. Two of the minor parties currently not only participate in the elective process, but contribute directly to the formulation of policy in the state's government. This is all achieved within a system of direct election of a single chief executive, plurality rule, single-member districts, two major parties, and other common features of American party systems.

## Third Parties in New York

The most important of New York's third parties are the Liberals and the Conservatives. The two are similar in the breadth of their appeal and oftentimes in their political behavior, but they have distinctly different origins and goals.

The Liberal party, the latest expression of a socialist-labor movement that for decades harbored the idea of an independent labor party in the United States, is a splinter from the American Labor party, which emerged in the 1930s to support Franklin Roosevelt without working through Tammany Hall. The Liberal party's ideological differences with its predecessors in the socialist-labor tradition often obscure the historical continuity. For instance, the Socialist Labor party rejects the entire capitalist concept of the political economy; the Liberal party does not. It rejects the idea of revolution, seeking to accommodate to the political realities of New York and the nation. The Liberal party's nonrevolutionary New Deal position has also provided a comfortable alternative for leftist intellectuals disenchanted with the excesses of the Communist party.

The Conservative party, in contrast, expresses a tradition of the Republican party that has been given scant respect within the party in recent years in New York. If Nelson A. Rockefeller represents the liberal progressive tradition in modern Republicanism, the Conservative party represents the contrary tradition associated with Robert A. Taft and Barry Goldwater. The founders of the Conservative party, while firmly committed to the two-party system, considered themselves the true representatives of Republicanism in New York. By going outside the Republican party, they hoped to force it to make conservative nominations and policy decisions in order to regain support from its conservative members. Specifically, the Conservatives wanted to release the Republican party from the control of Nelson Rockefeller. While they were never able to dislodge Rockefeller from the governorship, they nonetheless won enough votes to cause Rockefeller to move to the right.

BREADTH OF APPEAL

The Liberal party steadily lost enrollment in New York City from 1960 until 1969, when Mayor John V. Lindsay lost the GOP primary and ran for reelection on the Liberal ticket (see Table 5-1).[1] Only the Lindsay candidacy can explain the unusual reversal of the decline in the party's enrollment. The Conservative party, meanwhile, having qualified as a legal party in the 1962 gubernatorial election, increased its enrollment throughout the decade. The extensive campaign efforts behind James L. Buckley's 1968 bid for the U.S. Senate and successful drive for the office in 1970 are responsible for the party's growth.

1. A voter may elect to enroll in a legal political party at the time he registers to vote or at any other time. Party enrollment entitles the voter to vote in the primary elections of that party.

TABLE 5-1. *Third-Party Registration in New York State, Selected Years, 1960–71*

In thousands

| Year | Liberal party | | | Conservative party | | |
|---|---|---|---|---|---|---|
| | N.Y. City | Upstate | Total | N.Y. City | Upstate | Total |
| 1960 | 74 | 25 | 99 | — | — | — |
| 1962 | 66 | 22 | 88 | — | — | — |
| 1964 | 63 | 25 | 88 | 9 | 13 | 22 |
| 1966 | 61 | 26 | 87 | 27 | 27 | 54 |
| 1968 | 61 | 33 | 94 | 52 | 55 | 107 |
| 1969 | 77 | 32 | 109 | 53 | 54 | 107 |
| 1970 | 78 | 35 | 113 | 56 | 61 | 117 |
| 1971 | 87 | 51 | 137 | 58 | 71 | 129 |

Source: *Manual for the Use of the Legislature of the State of New York*, annual volumes, 1960–1972.

Enrollment figures unfortunately often prove to be a poor indicator of party voting. The 1968 election of a state court of appeals judge offers a unique and more direct measure of party identification. Adrian Burke was nominated by all four parties for the judgeship. Voters were thus presented with a choice of parties but not of candidates. The election is an excellent indicator of the electorate's division by party label; 44 percent of the vote received by Burke was Republican, 44 percent Democratic, 7 percent Conservative, and 5 percent Liberal.[2] By the end of the 1960s, then, the two leading third parties between them could claim the allegiance of approximately one-tenth of the electorate.

## Election Strategies in New York

The election laws of New York enable the parties to pursue a variety of strategies and thus provide the voters with a wide range of choice. In New York the party, not the candidate, establishes a ballot position, and more than one officially recognized party

2. The election returns showed 15 percent of ballots in the judgeship column "blank, void, and scattering." Using all ballots, rather than all votes cast for Burke, relative party strength is 37 percent Republican, 37 percent Democratic, 6 percent Conservative, 4 percent Liberal, and 15 percent unidentified.

may endorse a candidate.[3] The candidate is listed under each party heading. Consequently, a third party that endorses a major-party nominee does not have its name withdrawn from the ballot, but simply inserts the candidate's name in its own line. In the 1970 gubernatorial race, for example, the Republican candidate, Rockefeller, was endorsed by the Civil Service Independent party and the Democratic candidate, Arthur Goldberg, by the Liberal party, so that each appeared in two columns of the ballot.

As a rule the modified two-party system gives a third party the choice of benevolently offering its endorsement to a candidate of a major party, of punitively withholding it and running its own candidate, or of remaining neutral and not participating in the election. In most statewide contests in New York the Liberal party has offered its endorsement to the Democrats and the Conservative its endorsement to the Republicans, thus forming two fairly stable major–third-party coalitions. The Liberal party, in this situation, can act punitively toward the Democratic party by occasionally endorsing a Republican, and the Conservative party can act punitively by doing just the opposite. The major parties have a choice of being receptive to the third parties and accepting their endorsements, of rejecting third parties by refusing to consider their endorsements, or of remaining neutral. They also have the alternative of adopting a destructive posture: through their control of the legislature, major parties can enact laws that place obstacles in the path of third parties.

There can be rewards for both members of a winning coalition between a major party and a third party. For the major party the primary reward is the election of its candidate. The third party's reward is less direct and comes if the official elected acts in accord with its interests, or if its leaders are appointed to office. The third party is in the best position to assert its claim when it has contributed a critical number of votes to an elected official's plurality— when it can be plausibly argued that the major-party candidate

---

3. A member of one party may run in another's primary only with the other party's permission, a qualification incorporated in 1947 under the Wilson-Pakula law.

could not have been elected without the number of votes polled on the third-party ticket.

Voters also benefit under the modified two-party system. When a third party nominates its own candidate, it provides a clear alternative to the frequently similar major-party candidates. When the party forms a coalition with a major party, it usually advocates different programs and represents different interests within the electorate, giving the voter a chance to indicate the public policies closest to his preference. The incentive for candidates to marshal majorities or large pluralities that is characteristic of two-party systems is retained. But, in addition, voters are given a wide variety of programs and party positions from which to choose.

In other states, third parties usually face an all-or-nothing decision of joining with a major party or going it alone. If a third party endorses a major-party candidate, it is often required to relinquish its position on the ballot and simply encourage its supporters to vote for the major party. Most states have antifusion and party-raiding statutes that inhibit or prevent multiple endorsements. They may, for example, require that a candidate be eligible to vote in the primary in which he desires to run; be affiliated with the party on whose ticket he runs; state his party affiliation when submitting nominating petitions; take an oath averring party membership and support of its principles and nominees in the general election; be nominated by no party other than the one for which petitions are submitted; or be nominated by electors of the party to which he belongs.[4] Failure to meet the statutory requirements results in omission from the ballot. Since fusion tickets are often the most effective strategy a third party can follow, these requirements effectively deny the third party an accurate count of its contribution to a major-party candidate. The third party is forced to choose between fielding its own candidate or backing a major candidate and withdrawing its party name from the ballot, which has usually meant disbanding the party.

4. "The Constitutionality of Anti-Fusion and Party-Raiding Statutes," *Columbia Law Review*, vol. 47 (1947), p. 1208.

## THIRD-PARTY SURVIVAL

As in most other states a third party may develop in New York when a strongly committed minority finds itself alienated from either major party. But what happens if the divisive issues disappear, if only temporarily, or if a major-party candidate makes overtures to the minority? In New York a third party can endorse a sympathetic major-party candidate in hopes of gaining at least some of its goals through the normal mechanisms of government. In a later election it can turn about and nominate its own candidate. The important factor is the party's place on the ballot, which it retains as long as it receives a minimum number of votes in a gubernatorial election; it is a legally recognized organization and has an autonomous identity. Thus third-party members can bring pressure to bear in elections without having to start anew at each election. The third party becomes an ever-present participant in the party system, shifting into and out of coalitions with the major parties according to the candidates and issue positions offered by those parties.

## COALITIONS AND VOTING

Under the New York system the contribution of a third party to a major-party candidate is visible.[5] The crucial role of such added support in New York has been evident in both state and national elections. In the 1954 gubernatorial election W. Averell Harriman apparently was carried to victory by Liberal votes. His Republican opponent, Irving M. Ives, received 49.9 percent of the votes while Harriman won 44.9 percent as a Democrat and 5.2 percent on the Liberal ticket.[6] In the 1960 presidential contest the Liberals again came to the rescue of the Democrats, providing the winning

5. A covert endorsement is, of course, an exception to this rule. In the gubernatorial election of 1938, for example, "the Communist party did not nominate a candidate for Governor and its leaders supported [the Democratic nominee] Lehman. One might assume then that the party gave Lehman its 100,000 votes." Rupert Hughes, *The Story of Thomas E. Dewey* (Grosset and Dunlap, 1939), p. 290.

6. V. O. Key, Jr., *Politics, Parties, and Pressure Groups* (5th ed., Crowell, 1964), p. 277.

margin for John F. Kennedy. Richard M. Nixon, the Republican candidate, won 47.3 percent of the vote while Kennedy won 47 percent on the Democratic ticket and 5.6 percent on the Liberal (the Socialist-Labor candidate received 0.2 percent).[7] The voting percentages are not conclusive evidence that without Liberal endorsement these major-party contenders would have done less well, but it is difficult to believe that the Liberal endorsement was not accountable in part for the final vote. Most political observers and politicians believe the endorsement had an important impact.

Over the years the system has been flexible, with major–third-party coalitions coming and going, depending on the special circumstances of each election. While fairly stable Democratic-Liberal and Republican-Conservative coalitions have recently prevailed, in the twenty-three gubernatorial elections between 1910 and 1970 the Republican party's candidate was endorsed by one or more third parties on only four occasions, the Democrats' on nine. As for coalitions between third parties, the American party endorsed the Prohibition candidate in 1914, and in a few elections in the 1920s factions of the socialist left endorsed one another's candidates. Throughout the sixty-year period one of the more enduring minor parties, the Socialists, consistently pursued an independent course. In contrast the American Labor party (ALP), the Liberal party, and less often the Conservative party have endorsed major-party nominees.

The coalitions at the state assembly level also have varied. The Socialist and Communist parties of the 1920s and 1930s usually chose to run independently, but they formed coalitions with major parties in a small number of districts. On the other hand, the ALP, like the Liberals and Conservatives later, followed a far more balanced strategy—particularly between 1936 and 1942—coalescing with the Republicans almost as often as the Democrats, and running independently in only a little more than half of the contests they entered. The Liberal party, since its inception in the 1940s, has consistently formed coalitions, usually endorsing Democratic

7. Ibid.

candidates, just as the Conservatives have supported Republicans since the early 1960s. Both have endorsed a major-party candidate in roughly half the assembly districts every election.

On the local level, third parties are more likely to run candidates independently in areas where they are strong. The Liberal party is strongest in New York City; in 1970 it ran 42 state assembly candidates independently and endorsed 25 Democrats in the city, while running 23 candidates independently and endorsing 39 Democrats elsewhere. The Conservative party in its suburban stronghold ran 16 assembly candidates independently and endorsed 8 Republicans in 1970; upstate it ran 14 candidates independently and endorsed 34 Republicans; and in New York City it ran 34 candidates independently and endorsed 25 Republicans. The number of Democrats endorsed by the Conservatives and Republicans endorsed by the Liberals is extremely small (see Table 5-2).

The elections for state assemblyman in 1968 and 1970, summarized in Table 5-3 in terms of third-party strategy, give some notion of the power of third parties. Each district contest in the two elections is categorized by the kind of strategy that the third

TABLE 5-2. *Liberal and Conservative Party Endorsements of New York Assembly Candidates, by Location, 1966, 1968, and 1970*

| | Liberal endorsement of | | | | Conservative endorsement of | | | |
|---|---|---|---|---|---|---|---|---|
| Location and year | Republican | Democrat | Liberal | No endorsement | Republican | Democrat | Conservative | No endorsement |
| New York City | | | | | | | | |
| 1966 | 1 | 39 | 27 | 1 | 14 | 1 | 36 | 17 |
| 1968 | 1 | 30 | 36 | 1 | 29 | 1 | 30 | 8 |
| 1970 | 0 | 25 | 42 | 1 | 25 | 0 | 34 | 9 |
| New York City suburbs | | | | | | | | |
| 1966 | 3 | 14 | 7 | 1 | 0 | 1 | 19 | 5 |
| 1968 | 0 | 15 | 10 | 0 | 6 | 0 | 18 | 1 |
| 1970 | 0 | 13 | 10 | 2 | 8 | 0 | 16 | 1 |
| Upstate | | | | | | | | |
| 1966 | 3 | 30 | 12 | 12 | 17 | 1 | 22 | 17 |
| 1968 | 1 | 23 | 15 | 18 | 28 | 2 | 11 | 16 |
| 1970 | 2 | 26 | 13 | 16 | 34 | 2 | 14 | 7 |

Source: Same as Table 5-1.

TABLE 5-3. *Influence of Third Parties' Strategies on Election Outcome of Major Parties in New York Assembly Districts, 1968 and 1970*[a]

| Strategy and outcome | Number of assembly districts | | | | | |
|---|---|---|---|---|---|---|
| | Liberal-Democratic coalition | | | Conservative-Republican coalition | | |
| | *1968* | *1970* | *Repeat*[b] | *1968* | *1970* | *Repeat*[b] |
| Benevolent strategy | | | | | | |
|   Critical win[c] | 5 | 2 | 0 | 9 | 5 | 1 |
|   Win | 37 | 33 | 22 | 26 | 40 | 21 |
|   Loss | 28 | 33 | 15 | 28 | 21 | 10 |
| Punitive strategy | | | | | | |
|   Critical loss[c] | 3 | 2 | 0 | 3 | 3 | 1 |
|   Loss | 29 | 30 | 14 | 35 | 38 | 23 |
|   Win | 29 | 33 | 21 | 25 | 24 | 13 |

Source: Same as Table 5-1.

a. Third-party strategy could not be determined in three Liberal-Democratic coalitions in 1968 and two in 1970 and in two Conservative-Republican coalitions in 1968. The Liberal party failed to enter the 1968 election in sixteen districts and the 1970 election in fifteen districts; the Conservative party failed to file in twenty-four districts in 1968 and in seventeen in 1970.

b. The third party repeated its 1968 strategy in the 1970 election.

c. A critical win or loss is one in which the third party provided enough votes to decide the election.

party adopted toward its normal coalition partner and the outcome of the election. The benevolent strategy is the endorsement of the coalition partner's candidate, the punitive the entry of an independent third-party candidate or, infrequently, the endorsement of the opposition's candidate. The election outcome is critical when the third party's strategy appears to have provided the margin of votes that determined the outcome. The outcome is a straightforward win or loss by the major party if its contest was not decisively affected by the strategy of its normal coalition partner.

The similarity of the two third parties' performances in the assembly contests is striking. Both adopted roughly the same number of benevolent as of punitive strategies and with roughly the same effect on the results of their partners' elections. The two parties seem to have been playing the same kind of game at the

local level—just what the Conservative party leaders had set out
to do in the early 1960s.

The most surprising fact is the relatively small number of contests in which the third parties apparently made the critical difference between winning and losing. Actually, the numbers are substantial enough to cause alarm within the major parties. In 1968
third parties were critical in sixteen contests (in four districts both
third parties were critical). Those sixteen contests involved over
10 percent of the total. Third parties were critical in nine contests
in 1970, a decrease in the marginal importance of their votes but
still a significant factor in the election. More important in the 1970
election was the closeness of the outcome in several races to the
critical win or loss, a cause of serious concern to the major parties.

Perhaps more contests are not critically affected because most
assembly seats are relatively safe for one major party or the other.
Seats in the assembly were won by 60 percent or more of the vote
in 68 percent of the contests in 1954, 63 percent in 1958, 65 percent in 1962, 50 percent in 1964, 65 percent in 1966, and 70 percent in 1968. The assembly district contests are not nearly so competitive as statewide contests.

The assembly elections were most often affected by third parties
in New York City's suburbs and suburban-like areas of Queens
and Richmond counties. The Conservative party, for example, provided the critical margin of victory in 1968 in one election in Richmond, four on Long Island (Suffolk, Nassau, and Queens counties), and two in the northern suburbs (Rockland-Orange and
Dutchess counties); it also afforded the victory in urban contests
in Kings (Brooklyn) and Erie (Buffalo) counties. That pattern is
characteristic of both the Conservative and the Liberal performance
in 1968 and 1970.

## Challenges to the Modified System

The leaders of New York's major parties occasionally have been
placed in a precarious position by their state's modified two-party
system. Consequently, attempts have been made to alter the state's

election laws in order to curtail third-party activity. The state courts have been responsible for the system's survival against these assaults.

One of the earliest defenses of third parties came in 1896, when the state court of appeals declared unconstitutional a statute preventing party committees from naming candidates already nominated by other parties, but allowing party conventions to do so. The court argued that the statute, "avowedly designed to stop fusion movements, was an unreasonable and arbitrary limitation of the right to nominate qualified people for office."[8]

A second major assault came in 1911 when the New York legislature, under the domination of Tammany Hall, approved a bill to change the state's ballot so that "the name of any candidate nominated by two or more parties or independent bodies might appear in but one column of the ballot."[9] The court of appeals unanimously declared this provision grossly unfair and discriminatory. It saw the law as an attempt to withhold a ballot position for members of a coalition or fusion ticket and thus to submerge third parties within a major-party column. Under the proposed system voters would be unable to identify most third parties, rendering fusion campaigns far less viable.

Two decades later the court of appeals struck down a statute requiring that a person nominated by both an established party and an independent group appear only on the line of the organized party, unless the independent group had nominated candidates in 50 percent or more of the offices being contested.[10] The 1930 statute aimed at discouraging third parties by eliminating the possibility of voting for a major-party candidate under a third-party label.

The precedent of sustaining participation by third parties was to a degree reversed in a ruling upholding the Wilson-Pakula law of 1947, a law designed to curtail the activities of the American Labor

8. "The Constitutionality of Anti-Fusion and Party-Raiding Statutes," p. 1211.

9. "Notes on Current Legislation," *American Political Science Review*, vol. 6 (February 1912), p. 57.

10. "The Constitutionality of Anti-Fusion and Party-Raiding Statutes," pp. 1211–12.

party. The law required that a member of one party running on the ticket of another have the approval of a (quorum) majority of "the party committee representing the political subdivision of the office for which a designation or nomination is to be made, or of such other committee as the rules of the party may provide." An exception was made for New York City, where the approval must be by a majority of the combined county executive committees. The adoption of this law left ALP officeholders, including Vito Marcantonio, a congressman from New York City, without an automatic right to run on a major-party line as they had done previously.[11] As a result the two ALP state legislators were defeated in 1948; Marcantonio was able to win one more term in Congress by running on the ALP ticket alone.

Except for the Wilson-Pakula limitations, the rights of third parties have been sustained, and several such parties flourished throughout the 1950s and 1960s. Multiple endorsements continue between Democrats and Liberals, Republicans and Conservatives, and in a few instances between Republicans and Liberals. In the mid-1950s the Republican-dominated state legislature did attempt to modify the election laws to impede the type of major–third-party coalition that produced a Democratic-Liberal governor in 1954. However, W. Averell Harriman, the beneficiary of the coalition, vetoed this legislation in both 1956 and 1957.[12]

With the growing strength of the Conservative party in the late 1960s, the picture changed. Even before the election of James Buckley, the Conservative candidate, to the U.S. Senate in 1970, Governor Rockefeller was contemplating changes in the election law to make third-party participation more difficult. In his first ten years as governor, Rockefeller was not inclined to favor action directed against the third parties. He was then cultivating a liberal

11. Marcantonio had become a highly controversial figure in the state because of his alleged associations with communists. He was continually berated for voting the "party line" in Congress, and he repeatedly captured his district primaries, winning on the Republican, Democratic, and ALP tickets from 1940 through 1946. Hugh A. Bone, "Political Parties in New York City," *American Political Science Review*, vol. 40 (February 1946), p. 275.

12. Key, *Politics, Parties, and Pressure Groups*, p. 277.

image, making successful appeals to the traditionally Democratic labor unions, and even—according to one associate—contemplating the possibility of running on the Liberal party ticket as Republican Senator Jacob Javits was doing. After the 1968 election the governor took a turn to the right, adopting a hold-the-line attitude toward state expenditures and supporting cuts in welfare and education programs.

As Rockefeller faced reelection in 1970 for a fourth four-year term, he partially dissociated himself from the campaign of Republican-Liberal Senator Charles E. Goodell and allowed his campaign to be associated to some extent with that of James Buckley. Rockefeller and Buckley shared headquarters in some of the suburban areas around New York City, particularly in Suffolk County. Through a convenient—and perhaps intentional—quirk in the crowded New York City ballot the names of Rockefeller and Buckley appeared in the same column, although they were not running in the same party. Rockefeller ran with the endorsement of the Civil Service Independents, Buckley with the endorsement of the Independent Alliance. These two third parties were listed in a single column, one under the other, with the names of their respective candidates, Rockefeller and Buckley.

Whatever association there was between the Republican candidate for governor and the Conservative candidate for senator, it was merely a temporary expedient. For as the Conservatives grew in strength, the Republicans became increasingly hostile and more willing to launch an assault on the Conservative party, which meant an assault on third parties in general. In the early weeks of the 1971 session, legislative leaders were reported to be considering a change in the election law that would prohibit a candidate from being listed in more than one column,[13] a potentially crushing blow to all third parties. On the last day of the session the legislature passed a law that restricted the number of columns on which a candidate could appear. It provided that for all offices, other than statewide and judicial offices, candidates accepting the nomination

13. Carter P. Morsley, *New York Times*, Jan. 14, 1971; and Rowland Evans and Robert Novak, *New York Post*, Jan. 16, 1971.

of a legal party—Republican, Democratic, Liberal, or Conservative—could not receive the nomination of an independent group.[14] In effect, the leading third parties were able to thwart the attempt to eliminate their coalition-making ability. Other third parties, however, were not beyond the reach of the legislature. The bill was passed 139 to 10 in the assembly, with the support of all the members who had been elected on both the Republican and the Conservative lines.

But the law was not to stand the test of judicial scrutiny. A local third party, the predominantly black United Ossining party (UOP), took action in the courts to have the new law invalidated. Part of the UOP complaint was that the Conservative party, which had polled fewer votes in local elections than the UOP, would have the right to endorse major-party candidates and the UOP would not. A special three-judge federal panel ruled the law unconstitutional on the grounds that it violated the First and Fourteenth amendments. The court found the law "fatally defective because of its flagrant discrimination against independent bodies and candidates nominated by such bodies. . . . Such invidious discrimination cannot be tolerated under the Fourteenth Amendment." Once again the courts came to the rescue of third parties.

In addition to the major parties' challenges, one of the prominent third parties, the Conservatives, has openly sought to eliminate another minor party that began to infringe on its constituency base. The chairman of the Conservative party successfully chal-

---

14. The 1971 legislature took additional action that affected the efforts of independent groups—third parties other than the legally defined Liberal and Conservative parties—to get on the ballot. The number of petition signatures required for statewide office was increased from 12,000 to 20,000, including at least 100 signatures in each of half of the congressional districts in the state (which replaced the requirement of at least 50 signatures from each county). The new law would have made it more difficult for George Wallace to get on the ballot in 1972. Other parties such as the Socialist Workers, the Communists, and the Socialist Labor party will have greater difficulty getting on the ballot. An attempt to change the legal definition of a political party from 50,000 to 100,000 votes received in the previous gubernatorial election failed in the 1971 session. A bill that passed increased the number of signatures for the designation of statewide candidates in party primaries from 10,000 to 20,000 or 5 percent (whichever is less), making opposition to the choice of the party's state committee in the primaries more difficult.

lenged before the New York secretary of state the ballot petition of George Wallace's Courage party and kept it off the 1970 ballot. Third parties can be as possessive of their domains as the major parties are.

Conditions today are similar to those that brought about the restrictive legislative actions in the early twenties against the Socialists, the mid-thirties against the Communists, and the late forties against the ALP and the Liberal party. In each instance a third party began to threaten the existing political order. The major parties attempted to impede its progress with legal weapons. The state's modified two-party system has nevertheless survived and is still the system most receptive to third parties among the states. In fact, in New York elections during the past decade the number of durable third parties has increased from one to two, and fringe parties have continued to proliferate.

## Sharing the Rewards of Victory

It is always difficult to determine precisely the extent to which a third party is rewarded for its contribution to the victory of a major-party candidate. In 1970 "about 150 leading Liberals [were] employed by the city or the courts," providing "a major patronage prop" for the party's leader.[15] Liberals have held positions such as deputy mayor, commissioner of the housing authority, and deputy commissioner of transportation. These jobs, intimately connected with the shaping of administration policy, represent something more than mere patronage. Through them the Liberal party can infuse its ideals into the policymaking process.

These kinds of rewards are also at issue during campaigns. When Arthur Goldberg was running for governor on the Democratic ticket in 1970, he met with the leaders of the New Democratic Coalition to seek their support. The NDC campaign chairman reported that Goldberg had assured him that "he had no commitments on patronage or influence for the Liberal party within

15. Frank Lynn, *New York Times*, Aug. 9, 1970.

his administration, that all appointments would be strictly on merit."[16]

The Liberal party, like the major parties, apparently is patronage-oriented. The newer Conservative party appears less so. Nonetheless, the party in 1970 held a half-dozen jobs on joint legislative committees that were obtained through party members in the assembly, and one Conservative was vice-chairman of the Joint Legislative Committee on Housing and Urban Development.[17] The party had been offered patronage through the Republican-held office of the Richmond borough president but had refused.[18]

Outside New York City the Conservatives hold few jobs. Nowhere has the party done as well as the Liberal party has done in New York City in converting its electoral strength into a claim for patronage. This, of course, may be due more to the lack of demand for patronage jobs by Conservatives than to their availability.

POLICY IMPACT

One indication of the impact of the third parties in New York State is their participation in legislative policymaking. For example, in the 1965 session of the state legislature—the only recent session controlled by Democrats in both houses—the Democratic-Liberal mayor of New York, Robert Wagner, had an extraordinary amount of influence. Both the speaker of the assembly and the senate majority leader were beholden to Wagner for their positions.[19] During this session, moreover, much of the Liberal party's legislative philosophy was reflected in the New York City program, a great deal of which was enacted into law. The Liberals, if only indirectly, saw the programs that they advocated being carried

16. Clayton Knowles, *New York Times*, July 3, 1970.

17. Joint legislative committees are interim study committees with combined payrolls of over $2 million; they are filled with patronage appointments.

18. Interview with James O'Doherty, state treasurer of the Conservative party, Sept. 3, 1970.

19. They were the minority choices of their respective party conferences but were elected to their positions by Republican votes after an arrangement had been made between the governor, who needed votes for his sales tax, and the mayor, who needed increases in state aid to the city.

out. But Liberal support of winning candidates has not always resulted in programs to the Liberals' liking.

The Conservative party claimed to have had a substantial amount of legislative influence for the first time in the 1969 legislative session, the first since 1964 to be controlled by the Republicans. The 1968 election had produced an assembly with seventy-six Republicans, seventy-two Democrats, and two Conservatives (who ran on the Republican line as well). With such a precariously small margin the Republican leadership paid attention to the Conservative party, which besides the two members of its own party had endorsed thirty-three incumbent Republicans and one Democrat. Representatives of the Conservative party were invited to sit with the Ways and Means Committee to discuss possible budget cuts. From the point of view of the assembly leadership, the Conservative party had been co-opted. As viewed by the Conservatives, the Republicans had been compelled to take their demands seriously.

The 1970 elections again produced a closely divided assembly: seventy-seven Republicans, two Conservatives, and seventy-one Democrats. Eleven of the Republicans had run on the Conservative ticket, and the two Conservatives on the Republican ticket. The two Conservatives joined the Republicans in their party conference, as they had in the previous legislature. In the Senate the Conservatives had less influence; the Republicans controlled that house by thirty-three to twenty-four, and only one Republican had had Conservative endorsement. The influence of the Conservative party in this session is apparent. Despite the major party leaders' readiness to curtail the rights of third parties, the restrictive legislation that was passed excluded both the Conservative and Liberal parties.

Their ability to check the destructive tendency of the Republicans in all likelihood derives from the Republicans' need for the cooperation of the Conservatives in passing a variety of bills. For example, on the sales tax increase the Republicans were shy one vote of the seventy-six needed for passage. The votes of the two Conservative members with the majority Republicans assured passage. In the roll calls on the major appropriations bills the two Conservatives offered the same support. The Republicans had no votes to spare on the passage of their state purposes bill and their capital construction bill, and had one extra vote on the legislature and judiciary bill and three extra on the local assistance and debt service bills.

Their reliance on the Conservative party for these votes put the minor party in a position to extract concessions from the Republicans. On a number of other crucial matters the Conservatives acted as pivotal voters, again enhancing their party's strategic importance to the Republicans.

Although the Liberal and Conservative parties are of different origin and different persuasion, in behavior they are often almost indistinguishable from one another or from the major parties. Much of their time and energy is spent in organizing locally and competing in elections. In their legislative activities they become immersed in the day-to-day tasks of program development, bargaining, compromising, and ultimately coalition-building with the major parties. Both parties seek traditional political rewards, jobs and program implementation. In some key areas the party members vote as a bloc, as is the case with major parties, but this is not an ironclad rule. Their demands, while to the left or right of the major parties, are nonetheless negotiable as public policy is being formed. Both third parties have been fairly successful in maintaining the allegiance of a sizable constituency and an active core of party workers and officeholders and have become a part of the political process. When such parties have been given a chance to participate, they have been as capable of accepting the responsibility of power as any major party.

## Cross-filing Systems

The New York system is not the only method of modifying a two-party system. Over the years a few states, notably California, have allowed candidates to file in the primary of any or all parties without specifying party affiliation.[20] This cross-filing system can also be thought of as a modified two-party system. However, whereas New York's system enables active participation by more than two parties in the general election, cross-filing systems greatly reduce the importance of all political parties.

Cross-filing in California evolved from the reform movement led by Hiram Johnson and the Progressives in the early 1900s. The first victory in their drive against boss control of the party system was replacement of the convention nomination system with a state direct primary in 1909. After Johnson won the governorship in 1910 and the Progressives claimed many seats in the state legislature in 1912, they attempted to eliminate the political party, that hierarchical, boss-ridden, and corrupt institution they considered the major obstacle to good government. To this end they sought to make the entire election process nonpartisan. Although nonpartisan ballot and registration schemes met with failure, nonpartisanship of a sort was initiated at the primary level. In 1913 the party test for entry in a primary was abolished and contenders were allowed to cross-file without listing party affiliation on the primary ballot. With only slight modification this nonpartisan feature of the direct primary law remained intact until 1952.[21] The law was abolished altogether in 1959.

The cross-filing option was so popular that, between 1914 and 1956, 47 percent of all candidates for statewide office used it.[22] The rate of success of those cross-filing varied, but it was always high. Between 1940 and 1952, 68 percent of all offices in the state were effectively won in the primary through cross-filing.[23]

20. Cross-filing has been permitted in Maine, Maryland, Massachusetts, New York, and Vermont; see Dean E. McHenry, "Cross Filing of Political Candidates in California," *Annals of the American Academy of Political and Social Science*, vol. 248 (November 1946), p. 226.

21. The Hawson Amendment of 1917 provided that a cross-filing candidate would be eliminated from contention in the general election if he did not win his own party's primary. In 1918 James Rolph, Jr., a registered Republican who won the Democratic party primary but lost the Republican contest, was barred from the general election ballot.

22. Robert J. Pitchell, "The Electoral System and Voting Behavior: The Case of California's Cross-filing," *Western Political Quarterly*, vol. 12 (June 1959), p. 462.

23. Ibid., p. 464.

One of the major reasons for its popularity, especially with incumbents, was that cross-filing did not require the notation of party
affiliation with a candidate's name on the primary ballot. Hence
the voter could distinguish between candidates only by name. As
a rule this procedure benefited the incumbent who could make
himself well known during his tenure in office. In 1950, for example, over 90 percent of all successful cross-filers were incumbents.[24] When the primary law was modified in 1952 to include
party labels as well as candidate names, the crossing of party lines
by self-identified partisans greatly diminished. In the ten years before this amendment, 42 percent of the voters in state primaries
had intentionally or unintentionally voted for a candidate of a party
other than their own; the crossover dropped to 23 percent in 1954,
and to 16 percent in 1956.

Though cross-filing is an alternative to the rigid domination of
the party system by two, and only two, major parties because it
reduces the importance of the party label in elections, it has not
opened the election arena but instead has served the interests of
incumbents. In combination with California's stringent requirements for entering the general election as a third party, the cross-
filing system led to a party system dominated by incumbents. It
thus accomplished the opposite of the modified two-party system,
diminishing the role of political parties and working against the
efforts of minority factions to gain recognition and a hearing in
the electoral arena.

## Conclusion

The essential attribute of New York's modified two-party system is the options it provides to both individual voters and political parties. For the issue-oriented voter the presence of fairly durable third parties affords a greater variety of choices among party
platforms and candidates than does a two-party contest. Alternative
arenas are available for potential activists who find the major-party
organizations either preoccupied with winning office or dominated

24. Ibid., p. 471.

by an older generation of politicians. Furthermore, the system does not force voters to choose between "throwing their vote away" or voting for one of two major parties. The modified system allows third parties to retain their specialized constituencies while contributing to election outcomes through coalitions with the major parties. Finally, the ability of third parties to survive over time makes them vehicles for new issues and new programs that otherwise would have to await acceptance by a much broader audience before the major parties would address them. Thus, durable third parties, even more than the short-lived third parties that emerge in the present national two-party system, hold the potential for stimulating political discussion and compelling politicians in power to stay abreast of current public trends.

Changing the election laws of other states to replicate those of New York would not, of course, automatically generate third parties or placate those groups demanding new forms of political participation. But it would certainly tend to facilitate change.

☆

*Chapter Six*

☆

# THE PAST AND FUTURE
# OF THIRD PARTIES

THE TEN third parties most significant in U.S. presidential elections, beginning with the Anti-Masons of 1832 and including the American Independent party of 1968, burst upon the national scene, amassing an appreciable number of popular votes, and then withered away in a fashion that is now predictable. It should be assumed that, in the future, significant third parties will follow the same pattern.

Third parties have provided important, sometimes crucial, access to the electoral arena for voting minorities. This important representative activity should be encouraged. Laws governing access to the ballot should be standardized, and their inhibiting effects should be minimized. Furthermore, to facilitate the survival of the third parties, a modified two-party system should be adopted.

## *Factors in Third-Party Voting*

The emergence of significant third parties depends on the coincidence of four factors: severe national conflict over a few very important issues, a period of "crisis politics"; division of the electorate on one or more of these issues into at least one intense and estranged minority and a broad majority; rejection or avoidance of the position of the minority by both major parties, causing alienation of the minority; and a politician or political group willing to exploit the situation by initiating a new party. Such a combination assures an appreciable third-party vote.

The conditions, however, are cumulative; each is necessary for the next to operate. Hence, except in a period of crisis, politically active minorities will usually be absorbed by the major parties; seldom will they be drawn into a third party. If during a crisis the major parties take opposing positions, little leeway remains for a third party. Lacking a political crisis and an intense minority to appeal to, few politicians of repute will venture to lead a third-party effort. But in a period of crisis when a minority emerges and the major parties ignore it, significant third parties appear. Together, the four conditions are sufficient to produce a large third-party vote.

A single factor, the depression stage of the economic cycle, has often been described as the crucial cause of third parties, with the groups affected first and most acutely—the less prosperous yet politically sensitive farmers and industrial workers—flocking to the protest banner.[1] As the economy plummets into a depression and more and more persons become adversely affected, the argument goes, one or both of the major parties shift attention to the economic issue and propose remedial action. Hence, following the initial thrust of third parties, major parties undermine their cause.

But several third parties, particularly those that arose outside the era of rapid growth of the industrial system, defy such a rule. For example, it is difficult to characterize 1968 as a year of severe recession or depression, even though the economy was no longer expanding rapidly and undercurrents of economic discontent were present. George Wallace gained support first on the issue of race relations and second on the issue of war in Vietnam. The economic protest thesis is of limited use in understanding third parties that have emerged out of intense social, racial, or foreign policy controversies.[2] It touches only on one of the many causes of political

1. See Murray S. Stedman and Susan W. Stedman, *Discontent at the Polls* (Columbia University Press, 1950), especially chap. 5.

2. Karl Boughan argues "neither southern nor non-southern Wallaceism occurred principally in a rural setting and neither was due to economic depression.

crisis, and it fails to identify the intervening steps—the emergence
of an intense minority and its alienation from the major parties—
between the crisis and the third-party voting.

Third parties are sometimes described as largely the product of
very ambitious men who were thwarted within the major parties.
The candidates of the most significant third parties were all prominent politicians at the state or national level prior to their third-
party bid.[3] George Wallace, for example, served as the Democratic
governor of Alabama before and after his third-party candidacy
in 1968. With his presidential ambitions stymied within the national Democratic party, he turned his energies to the American
Independent party (AIP). Similarly, the 1924 Progressive candidate, Senator Robert M. La Follette, had been a prominent leader of
the reformist wing of the Republican party in Wisconsin and nationally for two decades before his third-party campaign. Finally,
three of the most prominent third-party contenders—Martin Van
Buren in 1848, Millard Fillmore in 1856, and Theodore Roosevelt
in 1912—had formerly been President of the United States.

The success of third parties is not attributable to the ambition
and zeal of their candidates, however. Politicians of ambition and
fame are the leaders of the Republican and Democratic parties
as well, as are all those anxiously awaiting the chance to serve as
standard-bearer of one of the major parties. The great number of
ambitious politicians who hold positions of statewide or national
leadership should create many significant third parties in every
election if personal ambition were the crucial variable. Why, for
instance, did Henry Wallace fail to generate widespread voter
support in 1948? As vice president under Franklin Roosevelt and
as cabinet officer under two presidents, Wallace had demonstrated
his drive for high political office. Moreover, throughout his career

---

Nonetheless, at the bottom of each, economic discontent preceded and went on to
color the political protest." "The Wallace Phenomenon: Racist Populism and
American Electoral Politics" (Ph.D. thesis, Harvard University, 1971), p. 68.

3. Howard R. Penniman, "Third Parties and the American Two-Party System:
Some Interrelations" (paper prepared for delivery at the 1970 annual meeting of
the American Political Science Association), pp. 11–12; Penniman is not an advocate
of the "ambition thesis."

he championed the cause of farmers and industrial workers, two constituencies that might have given him far more than the 2.4 percent of the popular vote he ultimately received.

The personal ambition of leaders is surely one element in the composition of third parties. Without a candidate—as well as an army of party workers—third-party votes would never materialize. The evolution of a significant party depends largely, however, on conditions beyond the leader's control—the presence of a political crisis and the seeming abandonment of an intense minority by the major parties. Hence, the zeal of a man like George Wallace would have been of little consequence without the divisive racial controversy of the 1960s.

Sweeping realignments, precipitated by social and political upheavals that render old party alliances untenable, are widely thought to encourage third parties. New sets of coalitions are sought within the major parties, but strong partisan ties complicate the shift. Disaffected groups, when withdrawing their support from the traditional parties, hesitate to coalesce with their long-standing adversaries and are thus open to appeals from other sources. Third parties appear in response to the needs of the disaffected transitional groups. Usually after one election has passed, the alternate major party actively courts the disaffected group and wins its confidence, spelling doom for the third party.

In the 1960s when the United States was undergoing unprecedented social and political upheavals, some observers saw a realignment of groups between major parties.[4] The AIP was then considered the refuge in the realignment of conservative Democrats in the South—and elsewhere—en route to an ultimate merger with the Republican party.[5]

The elections of 1912 and 1924, on the other hand, saw significant third parties that arose when no fundamental realignments were under way. Conversely, the most far-reaching realignment

4. Gerald M. Pomper, *Elections in America: Control and Influence in Democratic Politics* (Dodd, Mead, 1968).

5. Kevin P. Phillips, *The Emerging Republican Majority* (Arlington House, 1969).

of the twentieth century—the reshuffling of loyalties in the New Deal era—failed to produce a significant vote for a third party.

Third-party voting clearly has a number of necessary components. A period of crisis or an ambitious leader alone is insufficient. The crisis must occur in conjunction with the emergence of an intense minority or minorities, and their rejection by the major parties; only then, with ambitious leadership, can a significant third party emerge.

### PUBLIC OPINION AND PARTY STRATEGY

The contest for the presidency is considered central to the existence of the two-party competition in the United States. With a multiplicity of political factions, each attempting to become a part of the winning coalition, the number of effective contenders is reduced to two, the candidates of the two national major parties. With the major parties thus composed of diverse interests, the most viable position on issues is found by moving to the center, rather than appealing to the extremes.[6] If it is to succeed, a major party "must be supported by a great variety of interests sufficiently tolerant of each other to collaborate, held together by compromise and concession, and the discovery of certain common interests." Its managers must realize that they "need not," or more appropriately cannot, "meet every demand by every interest."[7]

In certain instances, however, moving to the center may not be the best strategy. To do so makes sense only when opinions are arrayed in a normal bell-shaped distribution or when they are almost equally distributed.[8] For example, given two parties, A and B, and a bell-shaped distribution, competition for the most votes compels both parties to seek the middle ground. If candidate A takes position $A_1$, candidate B is then free to take position $B_1$, and under the assumption that voters will support the party closest to themselves, B can expect the votes of a majority of the electorate.

6. Anthony Downs, *An Economic Theory of Democracy* (Harper and Row, 1957).

7. E. E. Schattschneider, *Party Government* (Rinehart and Winston, 1942), p. 85.

8. Robert A. Dahl, ed., *Political Oppositions in Western Democracies* (Yale University Press, 1966), pp. 371–80.

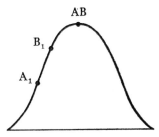

The party that is closer to the center may expect to win a majority vote. Thus, the center is the only viable position for both parties. In practice, each major party has striven to establish itself as the party of the center, while attempting to make the other's position appear to be extreme.

The same is true when opinions are more or less equally distributed. Any move away from the center by one party leaves the

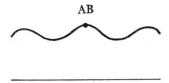

other an opportunity to fill the void between itself and the first party, thus winning the support of the majority.

These customary patterns of public opinion can be accommodated within the framework of two-party politics. The split in public opinion that occurs when views on fundamental issues polarize is not so easily resolved. With voters solidifying into two fairly equal and distinctive camps, moderation is replaced by conflict and confrontation. In these instances of intense political crisis the two parties, "each striving to retain the support of the extremists on its flanks, will only exacerbate a conflict."[9]

In such a situation the existing political parties must either change their strategies or lose ground to new and more aggressive parties;

9. Ibid., p. 376.

the fence-straddlers, mollifiers, and compromisers invariably lose to the dogmatic, aggressive zealots. Neither can opt for the center position, AB, for new parties will surely appear on the left and right ex-

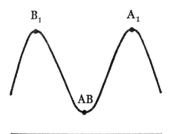

tremes, taking strong stands and appealing to large numbers of voters. If both opt for one side of the issue, they risk leaving the opposing view, which appeals to roughly half of the electorate, to a new party to exploit. If the divisive issues dominated the election, the new party would be an almost certain winner in a three-party contest. Probably each major party will move to that side of the issue it has traditionally leaned toward, with each becoming an avid champion rather than a middle-of-the-roader. For example, if the electorate split into two fairly equal groups on a divisive economic issue, the Democratic party could be expected to shift to a more liberal position, say, to $B_1$, and the Republicans to a more conservative stance, $A_1$. In this case politics would probably not remain low-keyed, moderate, or compromise-oriented, but, nonetheless, the contest could be expected to remain two-party.

When a vast majority of the electorate is at one extreme and an intense minority at the other, the major parties are again unable to take the centrist position, AB. The presence of intense conflict

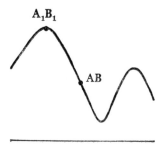

demands that parties choose sides. But when the majority is on one side of an issue, the major parties are not likely to take up the different sides. Neither can champion the minority view and expect to carry the election. Thus the two compete for the votes of the vast majority, seeking the middle range of the majority side of the conflict—position $A_1B_1$.

In this situation a third party can enter the political arena with the likelihood of receiving appreciable support. The third party quite logically emerges to champion the intense and estranged minority. Again, the cumulative effect of four factors—a few highly salient issues, the way they divide the electorate, the response of the major parties, and the presence of an organizing agent to mobilize the minority—accounts for a significant third-party vote.

### THE WITHERING OF THIRD PARTIES

Even more predictable than the emergence of significant third parties is their demise. Neither the AIP nor any other significant third party has in later competition with the two major parties bettered its initial popular vote. Nor is any likely to do so in the future without appreciable changes in the electoral system. The consistent decline is principally due to the increased efforts of the major parties. Usually after a strong showing by a minor party, at least one of the major parties shifts its position, adopting the third party's rhetoric if not the core of its programs. Consequently, by the following election the third-party constituency has a choice between the "extremist" third party with little hope of victory and a major party more sympathetic to its needs.

Once the major parties begin to undermine the third party's positions on one or two divisive issues, the third party is at a disadvantage. The major parties have the organizational resources, deep-rooted party attachments, moderate and reasonable image, and access to governmental institutions needed to deliver on campaign promises. They also can offer the hope of patronage and other rewards. Meanwhile the fervor aroused by the third party when it entered the two-party system is difficult to sustain; early partisans often return to one of the major parties. The image of extremism that remains in the public's mind restricts the third party's ability to extend its appeal to the mainstream of voters; despite efforts to do so, Wallace could not shake his antiblack image in 1972.

Often third parties lose ground because of shifts in public concern. As social, economic, and political changes occur—as the intensity of a political crisis subsides—so does the prominence of any one or two issues. Thus a third party that in one election gained attention with a highly visible and divisive issue may find itself irrelevant and ignored four years later.

## A Black Third Party

Although the general pattern of emergence and decline has held for all significant third parties, the particulars of each party movement have varied. Just as the core issues in each period of severe political crisis have differed, so too have the estranged groups whose sympathies the third parties have gained.

The most potent contemporary issue that might precipitate another period of intense national conflict and with it the likelihood of significant third parties is racial cleavage. While the issue has already been exploited to foster third parties among whites, most recently by the AIP, and may be again, blacks have yet to mount such a drive.

The absence of national third-party activity among blacks may be attributable to their sympathetic treatment from segments of the white population. The racial issue has not rigidly divided the population into the white majority and black minority, with both major parties appealing to the white majority. Consequently, although the conflict has been intense, an estranged black minority party has not evolved.

In addition, blacks have been hampered in a number of ways. They have lacked the resources and freedom necessary for establishing autonomous political organizations. In the past, whites, operating a political system under conditions of continuing racial conflict, solved their problem "by the simple expedient of disfranchising the weaker of the two clashing groups—by creating a mixed system of democracy for whites and autocracy for Negroes."[10] Such a dual system made the likelihood of an explicitly black-oriented party remote. Until recently these deterrents to independent black action have been inhibiting in the North, and prohibitive in the South.[11] The pattern is changing, however, and the potential for an independent black party exists.

THE POTENTIAL FOR A BLACK PARTY

Clearly, blacks will continue to press for an equitable share of economic and social advantages in American society. Since many of these gains will come from resources and privileges whites now control, conflict along racial lines is bound to continue. Should the issue explode into the divisiveness, confrontation, violence, and extended period of crisis experienced in the 1960s, and should the major parties ignore or actively repudiate the black minority, a successful third-party movement is likely.

Blacks, with resounding increases in voter registration in recent years, particularly in the South,[12] now have the base for a successful third-party vote. With 10 percent of the eligible national electorate nonwhite, the bulk of them having access to the polls, and with these votes largely concentrated in key urban states, an independent black party movement could have a dramatic impact on national elections. Moreover, black politicians now can provide experienced leadership for such a party. Between 1968 and 1970 the number of black elected officials increased by 30 percent, and blacks had won in 1,860 national, state, and local offices.[13] Some of these officeholders are persuaded of the power to be gained

10. Donald R. Matthews and James W. Prothro, *Negroes and the New Southern Politics* (Harcourt, Brace and World, 1966), p. 472.

11. See Hanes Walton, Jr., *The Negro in Third Party Politics* (Dorrance, 1969).

12. From 1940 to 1970 black registration in the eleven southern states rose from 5 percent to 66 percent of those eligible. Matthews and Prothro, *Negroes and the New Southern Politics*, table 1-1, p. 18; and "Voter Registration in Southern States," *Congressional Quarterly Weekly Report*, vol. 27 (Dec. 11, 1970), p. 2952.

13. Joint Center for Political Studies, "National Roster of Black Elected Officials" (Washington, D.C., March 1971; processed).

through unified black action, as evidenced by the black caucus formed in Congress in 1970.[14]

Not only do blacks have more power; they have also become exceedingly issue-oriented when racial issues appear in campaigns. This was demonstrated in the overwhelming support given Carl B. Stokes and Richard D. Hatcher by blacks in mayoralty elections in 1967.[15] One of the most revealing instances of the flexibility of black voters was the split-ticket voting by an astonishing 72 percent of all blacks who voted in two Senate races in Virginia in 1966: in one contest the moderate Democrat William Spong received 91 percent of the black vote, while in the other the conservative Democrat Harry F. Byrd, Jr., won only 19 percent.[16] Similar dramatic shifts in expressing their interests—"voting black" —have occurred between consecutive elections. Blacks in Georgia voted 96 percent Democratic in the 1964 presidential contest (two points higher than the black support for Johnson nationwide) but a mere 18 percent Democratic for the segregationist Lester Maddox two years later in the gubernatorial race. In Arkansas the black vote went from 14 percent for the Republican presidential candidate in 1964 to 71 percent for Republican Governor Winthrop Rockefeller in 1966. Regardless of the contest, black voters show greater shifts between parties than virtually any other group in the electorate. When racial prejudice or segregation is the theme of a major party contender, no call to party allegiance can countermand the racial solidarity of the black community.

Black independence from the major parties is not apparent in recent national voting patterns. With the nonwhite vote reportedly at 94 percent and 85 percent Democratic in the 1964 and

14. See William Raspberry, *Washington Post*, Dec. 4, 1971.

15. Jeffrey K. Hadden, Louis H. Masotti, and Victor Thiessen, "The Making of Negro Mayors 1967," *Trans-action*, January–February 1968, pp. 21–30. See also Pat Watters and Reese Cleghorn, *Climbing Jacob's Ladder: The Arrival of Negroes in Southern Politics* (Harcourt, Brace and World, 1967), pp. 83–85; and William Brink and Louis Harris, *Black and White: A Study of U.S. Racial Attitudes Today* (Simon and Schuster, 1966), chap. 4.

16. The second vacancy arose because of the resignation of Harry Flood Byrd, Sr.

1968 elections[17] and similarly high in 1972, little flexibility seems to exist. But this is an unwarranted conclusion, for the national Democratic leadership has taken care not to offend the black community.

### THE PRICE OF INDEPENDENCE

If the first three conditions of third-party voting should again be met, the black community now has access to the polls and the available leadership necessary for a significant third-party vote. Any black third-party movement would, however, run contrary to the usual patterns of electoral politics. Except in the event of intense confrontation between the races, incentives exist for blacks and whites to form coalitions in pursuit of their common objectives. Thus in most instances the price of following an independent party route is more than blacks are willing to pay. In either a plurality or a majority system a black third party may do no more than siphon off votes from the major-party candidate who is more responsive to black interests, thereby ensuring victory for the candidate most opposed to black interests.[18] Moreover, to withdraw from the Democratic party would probably mean an end to its patronage for blacks, to black influence within that party, and to the accumulated seniority of black Democrats within Congress. The fact remains that the primary needs of the black community are more jobs, better schooling, and better housing, and they can best be met by gaining political power through coalition politics in the electoral arena.[19]

## An Ecology Party

Race now is unique as a festering national issue with the potential for generating divisive controversy, an estranged minority, and

17. Richard M. Scammon and Ben J. Wattenberg, *The Real Majority* (Capricorn ed., Coward, McCann and Geoghegan, 1971), p. 345.
18. See Watters and Cleghorn, *Climbing Jacob's Ladder*, p. 342.
19. See Bayard Rustin, "Mobilizing a Progressive Majority," *New Leader*, Jan. 25, 1971, pp. 7–10.

significant third-party activity. Among other compelling national
issues, environmentalism is a cause that in the foreseeable future
may develop that potential.

Environmentalists find little sympathy for their demands for
fundamental change in the methods of production and patterns of
consumption among the political leaders of the nation, who stress
economic growth. With the increasing rate of water and air pollution and accelerating consumption of scarce natural resources,
many environmentalists believe that both the current and future
generations are endangered. But there are no simple solutions to
these problems. Effective pollution controls are costly, shifting to
new systems of production and materials will antagonize many
powerful and vested interests, and any attempt to impose restrictions on a consumption-oriented public will be met with strong
resistance. The major parties are aware of both the need for change
and the difficulty of achieving anything but minimal adjustments.
Both have endorsed programs to protect the environment and re-
verse the present trend, but both continue to sanction the modes of
production and consumption at the root of environmental decay.

Equivocation and faith in incremental adjustment will not satisfy
intensely committed environmentalists if conditions steadily worsen.
Such a trend, combined with some catalytic event—for example,
an explosion in one of the growing number of nuclear energy
plants in the United States—could conceivably precipitate the appearance of an ecology party in national politics. Quite probably,
it would gain prominence by challenging the two major parties in
a presidential contest, then in subsequent years throw its support
to either the Republicans or Democrats. Short of such an extreme
occurrence, it is likely that the incremental approach now being
pursued by the major parties will forestall that degree of alienation
necessary for third-party activity.

## The Third-Party Impact

Third parties crystallize issues that might otherwise go unheeded
or receive little attention during a campaign. If nothing else, they

serve an educational function in drawing attention to neglected issues and proposing new and sometimes radical solutions, some of which eventually are adopted by the major parties. But in raising issues they do not topple the entire democratic system or generate a chain reaction of more and more third parties.

In gaining implementation of their programs, their success is mixed. Sometimes they are quite successful, sometimes not. A key element in these variations appears to be whether the third party reflects the views of a growing cause or a dying minority. When the parties champion views that are the wave of the future such as electoral reform, progressive taxation, abolition, or antibusing, they can justly be portrayed as the vanguard of change, articulating issues and laying the groundwork for the programs the major parties ultimately carry out. If, however, they represent views on passing issues or those that are rapidly declining in adherents, they may at best slow the pace of change, but little will come of their substantive proposals. Which is only to say that the U.S. political system is basically majoritarian and, in order to see their programs implemented, third parties must await the spread of their ideas among a wider public, and adoption of those ideas by the larger parties.

Part of the adoption process, indeed a crucial part, is the potential contribution of the third party's constituency to one of the major parties in a forthcoming election. For instance, both Cleveland and McKinley appear to have considered the Populists of little consequence to their eastern-based coalitions. Nixon, on the other hand, seems to have considered the support of the AIP constituency important to a Republican presidential victory in 1972. Thus he sought to appease the anti-integration forces.

In terms of affecting the course of elections, third parties have rarely denied victories by drawing off votes from traditional-party candidates who would have won otherwise. Rather consistently they have had a marginal impact on the composition of the electorate. By bringing new and otherwise uninvolved citizens to the polls they generate new interest among some segments of the population. Meanwhile, the relative sameness of the major-party contenders in three-way contests gives their partisans less incentive than usual to vote, and an appreciable number of the major-party constituents stay home on election day. Thus in the aggregate the proportion of voters usually declines in three-party contests.

Third parties are not necessarily progressive and innovative, yet neither are they unproductive or counterproductive. They do have a strong impact on American democracy. On these grounds their opponents contend that third parties should be discouraged. Though third parties do disrupt "politics as usual," they clearly are not undemocratic. They provide a voice for minorities that would otherwise go unrepresented in the most democratic of arenas, elections. Third parties are the primary means in the electoral system for dissatisfied citizens to challenge the reigning major parties. While this means has been used only on occasion, the mere fact of its existence provides an important check on the performance of the two major parties.

The question of third parties' role, then, is essentially one of whether the party system should be open to all contenders, allowing for free expression and with it the introduction of new ideas and issues into the political dialogue. The alternative is a system predominantly restricted to the two existing major parties. To restrict the free development of third parties because of their discomforting short-term effects is to rely exclusively on the Democratic and Republican parties to represent the wants and needs of all Americans. The interests of the American people are too diverse for two parties to do this adequately all the time. Moreover, the major parties can and do make mistakes. Their performance is likely to be most satisfactory, therefore, when they live in danger of displacement by new parties.

## Broadening Participation in the Electoral Arena

Democratic principles are best served when the electoral system encourages the presentation of all points of view rather than when it obscures all but middle-of-the road positions. Third parties help broaden participation by providing the electorate with a wide range of views and candidates at little cost to the integrity and viability of the electoral system. But third parties have traditionally been short-lived. Even when they have been able to hurdle the legal barriers and enter the politicial arena in times of crisis, they have been unable to sustain their important representative function in the day-by-day, year-in-year-out national political process. Greater independent representation, expression of diverse views, and wider choice of candidates could be made possible by a greater accommodation of minority parties.

### A FEDERAL ELECTION CODE

A new party seeking a ballot position in the presidential contest must qualify state by state, encountering a wide variety of filing dates, petition requirements, loyalty oaths, and so on. Some state regulations, such as requiring petitions with signatures from 10 percent or more of the electorate to qualify for a position on the ballot, serve more as prohibitions to entry than as guarantees of orderly elections. The most direct and practical method of countering such problems is through the establishment of national requirements for access to the presidential ballot.

A federal election code should standardize electoral procedures in all the states and territories. The procedures, moreover, should be few and simple. The petition requirement should be no more than 1 or 2 percent of the electorate, the filing date no more than two months away from the election. This would eliminate the onerous petition requirements, the wide spread in filing dates, high filing fees, cumbersome organizational requirements, and loyalty oaths that new and small parties now face.

Once on the ballot, third parties should be provided with publicly sponsored television and radio broadcasting time. At least some hearing for the ideas and programs of other than the major parties should be ensured. Publicly sponsored media time for every qualified party could be incorporated into a federal election code either through the Voter's Time plan proposed by the Commission on Campaign Costs in the Electronic Era, or according to an Equal Time plan that would provide a minimal amount of publicly sponsored time, such as four half-hour periods.[20] In either case, new and small parties would be assured of a limited degree of mass media exposure.

### THE MODIFIED TWO-PARTY SYSTEM

If the electoral system is to support an ongoing dialogue that is not limited to the major parties, the system must be adjusted to allow some third parties to participate actively in more than a single election. The modified two-party system makes that possible. Under a modified system third parties are sparked by the same kinds of racial, economic, or other cleavages as under the present system. Yet the modified system provides more than just the opportunity for minorities to find independent expression in the heat of controversy; it enables them to survive.

The modified system, as it operates in New York State, provides a column on the ballot for each party in conjunction with the option of multiple-party endorsements. Third parties are able to survive by endorsing major-party candidates on some occasions and for some offices, while fielding their own candidates and programs on others. Third parties need not forsake their independent organization, identity, and ballot position, then, in order to support a major-party candidate when they deem conditions appropriate. Instead, a third party simply places the name of the major-party contender in its own column on the ballot. Over the years the system has resulted in a variety of party coalitions in New York, most frequently the Liberal party endorsing statewide Democratic candidates and the Conservative endorsing Republicans.

The critical advantage of the modified system is the continuing presence of third parties that represent alternative policies and whose political perspectives are distinctively different. Third parties taking strong policy positions would provide a counterbalance to the major parties' tendencies to equivocate, to opt for the center on every issue, and to give little attention to long-term planning and the development of coherent programs. This is not to expect that the major parties would adopt polar positions.

20. See Chapter 4, pp. 107–10.

Rather, with the third party's explicit programs and political views at the fringe, each major party would have to move incrementally away from dead center to avert defections to the third party.

These small moves could help to ensure that the vast majority of the electorate were presented with sharp differences between the major parties on pressing political issues. The more active participation of third parties under the modified two-party system would provide a continuing check on the major parties rather than the potential but seldom realized check under the present system. Third parties able to survive beyond the crisis that gave rise to them provide a readily accessible means for constructively channeling discontent, unrest, and dissent into the political arena. In short, an early warning system would exist for emergent crises. Through their active participation well beyond a crisis period, third parties might help to bring about changes in a gradual and constructive manner. The dependence on crises to alert public and political leaders to the need for change might be replaced by a system that provides for continual airing of minority views and prodding of the major parties by independent parties.

# Conference Participants

WILLIAM NISBET CHAMBERS *Washington University*
RONALD FORMISANO *University of Rochester*
FRED I. GREENSTEIN *Wesleyan University*
WILLIAM R. KEECH *Brookings Institution*
DONALD J. MCCRONE *University of Iowa*
DONALD R. MATTHEWS *Brookings Institution (Chairman)*
DAVID R. MAYHEW *Yale University*
DANIEL A. MAZMANIAN *Brookings Institution*
JUDITH H. PARRIS *Brookings Institution*
HOWARD R. PENNIMAN *Georgetown University*
MAURICE PINARD *McGill University*
JERROLD G. RUSK *Purdue University*
GILBERT Y. STEINER *Brookings Institution*
HANES WALTON, JR. *Savannah State College*
STUART K. WITT *Skidmore College*

# Index